"At a time when some fear that confession of sin will be a turnoff to the gospel, Duguid and Houk show how the heart longing for reconciliation with God can find peace and beauty in biblical confession. Long ago, another wrote that grace is not sweet if sin is not bitter. Duguid and Houk help us face the bitter to taste the sweet."

—**Bryan Chapell**, Senior Pastor, Grace Presbyterian Church, Peoria, Illinois

"When Scripture is scattered like seeds into good soil, a garden grows. This book is a fruitful garden, the fruit of good soil—fragrant, nutritious, beautiful. It calls us into the light, humbles us in our varied needs, delights us in God's many mercies. It is a resource for worshiping honestly and well. And it is a resource for living honestly and well. And it is a resource that will bless you when you put it to work."

—**David Powlison**, Faculty Member, Christian Counseling and Educational Foundation (CCEF), Glenside, Pennsylvania

"This book has many virtues. One is its flexibility in being adaptable to a range of situations, including public worship and private devotions. Another is the careful thought that went into the individual prayers. A third virtue is the rootedness of the individual units in Bible passages. Finally, the table of contents shows at a glance that the book covers the whole of the Christian life. I love the overall aims and method of this book, as well as the execution of details."

—**Leland Ryken**, Professor of English, Wheaton College, Wheaton, Illinois

"I find it easier to learn about God than to talk to him. These devotional prayers assist me in doing both, with the added benefit that they inspire me to pray those prayers with others."

—**Edward T. Welch**, Faculty Member, CCEF, Glenside, Pennsylvania

PRONE TO WANDER

PRONE TO WANDER

PRAYERS OF CONFESSION AND CELEBRATION

BARBARA R. DUGUID AND
WAYNE DUGUID HOUK

EDITED BY IAIN M. DUGUID

P&R
PUBLISHING
P.O. BOX 817 • PHILLIPSBURG • NEW JERSEY 08865-0817

ISBN: 978-1-59638-879-6 (pbk)
ISBN: 978-1-59638-880-2 (ePub)
ISBN: 978-1-59638-881-9 (Mobi)

Printed in the United States of America

Library of Congress Control Number: 2014946089

To Iain/Dad, with love and gratitude for your outrageous patience and kindness to us, and for enduring this process hopefully. Thanks for loving us, bringing out the best in us, and being our steady Doozer.

O to grace how great a debtor
Daily I'm constrained to be!
Let thy goodness, like a fetter,
Bind my wandering heart to thee.
Prone to wander, Lord, I feel it,
Prone to leave the God I love;
Here's my heart, O take and seal it,
Seal it for thy courts above.

—Robert Robinson, 1758

CONTENTS

FOREWORD

Confession is good for the soul. Certainly, historic liturgies shaped by the gospel always featured corporate confession as a central element.* In this they were simply following the biblical pattern of passages like Daniel 9 and Nehemiah 9. Yet these historic and biblical patterns have in many cases disappeared from our contemporary worship services. Some have become uncomfortable with the explicit language of sin, replacing it instead with more therapeutic and positive messages. When we do that, though, we remove the heart of the gospel, eviscerating everything that makes it really good news. If it is not clear what we have been saved from, why is it so tremendous that we have been saved?

Likewise in our own personal devotional lives, many of us have an ambiguous relationship to confession. We may acknowledge that confession ought to be part of our pattern of prayer, in line with the teaching of Jesus' model prayer, "Forgive us our debts, as we also have forgiven our debtors" (Matt. 6:12). Yet for many of us, much of the time, we find that either our prayers of confession are rather shallow and general, or they become mind-numbingly repetitive, confessing the same failings over and over again.

These were the problems that we encountered when we started putting together the order of worship for Christ Presbyterian Church in Grove City, Pennsylvania. We began by using a number of historic prayers of confession, drawn from the Book of Common Prayer and other fine old liturgies. But we soon found that these general prayers of confession were, well, rather general. There is nothing wrong with "acknowledging and bewailing our manifold sins and wickedness" or confessing the fact that we have

* Bryan Chapell, *Christ Centered Worship* (Grand Rapids: Baker, 2009), 89.

"left undone those things which we ought to have done and have done those things that we ought not to have done,"* but what exactly are these things that we admit that we have done or not done? If we are "to confess our particular sins particularly," as the Westminster Confession of Faith suggests (15.5), shouldn't our prayers of confession have a bit more particularity to them? So Wayne and Barb started writing particular and specific prayers of confession to go with our service, closely allied with the particular theme of that week's service. We soon discovered that people were taking home the bulletin after church was over and using these prayers in their own devotional lives on a daily basis. We began to recognize that there might be a wider audience for these prayers, both among people tasked with putting together services for their churches and with individuals seeking help for their own private or family devotional life.

The structure of these confessions is straightforward. We begin with a scriptural call to confession, which roots and grounds our confession in God's Word. Some whose consciences are overactive may be inclined to confess actions and attitudes that are not in themselves sinful, while others of us need to be confronted with Scripture to see the reality of the sin to which we so easily grow blind. The Bible is to be our sole rule of faith and practice, and the scriptural call to confession underlines that reality. In many cases the prayers themselves are explicitly Trinitarian, confessing our many failings to the Father, giving thanks to the Son for his death on the cross as well as for his perfect (and specific) obedience in our place which is credited to us by faith, and then asking the Holy Spirit to strengthen us to pursue lives of new obedience.

Of course, the purpose of confessing our sins is not to render us miserable by simply reminding us what great sinners we are. It is to remind us of what a great Savior we have. We confess that "there is no health in us" in order that our hearts may be drawn afresh to the Great Physician of our souls, who has provided for our desperate need for cleansing in the gospel. For that reason, we always follow

* The language of both quotes comes from the 1662 Anglican *Book of Common Prayer.*

our prayer of confession with a scriptural assurance of pardon: God's authoritative declaration of the forgiveness of each and every one of the sins of his people in Jesus Christ. This is our only hope in life and death. These assurances, too, we have endeavored to make specific, providing gospel encouragement tailored to our particular failings and pointing us afresh to the new life that is ours in Christ.

With a view to use in private devotions, we have provided ninety-three prayers, which represent about three months' worth of daily readings. After that, it would be possible to return to the beginning and repeat the cycle. We have also added indexes of themes, Scriptures cited, and the sermon passages that gave us the focus for these particular prayers. We have suggested hymns or songs to accompany each prayer, representing the music that went with the prayers in their original worship context as well as allusions to hymns and songs within the prayers themselves. In this way, we have sought to give additional help for worship leaders, as well as resources for supporting personal devotion.

Our vast debt to others in this compilation should be evident to all. In particular, Arthur Bennett's *Valley of Vision** was inspirational for us, in both its scope and its rich and evocative language of devotion. We stand on the shoulders of giants who have gone before us, whose shoelaces we are not worthy to fasten. My teaching assistant at Grove City College, Clint Estes, proved once again to be an excellent and eagle-eyed editor, helping with drafting the material and saving me from many mistakes. We are also indebted to the team at P&R, and especially Amanda Martin, for many hours of hard work in helping us bring this material to its final form.

It is our prayer that God will continue to use these prayers in the lives of many people, so that we may once again rediscover that, as Martin Luther put it in the first of his ninety-five theses, "the entire Christian life is to be one of repentance."

Iain M. Duguid

* Arthur G. Bennett, *The Valley of Vision: A Collection of Puritan Prayers and Devotions* (Edinburgh: Banner of Truth, 1975).

ACKNOWLEDGMENTS

I would like to thank my husband, Iain, for working hard once again to bring order out of chaos and keep us moving forward with this book. His gentle leadership, sharp mind, and editing super-skills were a rich blessing to us. I also want to thank him for creating the context in which Wayne and I could work together and explore different concepts for corporate prayer in worship. Iain planted Christ Pres., which would become the catalyst and context for writing these prayers, and he hired the ridiculously bright and talented young man who became our son as we lived and ministered together.

I had the rich privilege of becoming Wayne's assistant in his work as music director for our church. It rapidly became evident to me, to Iain, and to everyone worshiping with us that God had given wonderful and unusual gifts to this young man, who was just twenty-five at the time. We still marvel today at how God used Wayne to shape the liturgy and worship of our church. Both are simple yet deeply profound, stirring both mind and heart with rich, life-transforming truth from beginning to end. Church planting was the crucible in which we sinned against one another, with pressure abounding and tempers flaring. And each Sunday morning, we gathered for worship and marveled once again at God's faithfulness in providing a rich abundance of all that we needed to help God's family to worship him with joyful awe and reverence. Each service was a grand celebration of how Christ has rescued us from our sin and given us himself. Through our work at Christ Pres., we began to learn the life of honest confession and continual repentance that continues to characterize our church and family life.

I would like to thank all the rest of our precious kids, Jamie, Sam and Peggy, Hannah, Rob, and Rosie, who are enthusiastic worshipers of Jesus Christ and have contributed many hours of labor and encouragement to our church over the years. When I have felt discouraged by my huge mountains of sin, they have reminded me, skillfully and faithfully, that the righteousness of Christ is big enough and strong enough to rescue a mom and pastor's wife as weak and sinful as I am. Their joy in Christ and endless forgiveness is more than I could have ever hoped or longed for, and I must say with all my heart that God has been more than faithful to these covenant kids. To God alone be the glory for his work in their lives.

Barbara R. Duguid

These confessions flowed organically out of relationship and a growing understanding of God's calling to live righteous lives, of our incredible capacity as humans to keep on sinning against him and others anyway, and of God's unchanging determination to seek after desperately wicked sinners and faithfully change them through the powerful work of Christ's life, death, and resurrection. Primarily, I owe thanks to my adopted mom and dad, Barb and Iain Duguid, who had the guts to take in a confused, scared, and emotionally messy twentysomething and teach me the gospel story in all its earthy richness through practical love and investment in my life. I will be forever grateful for your sincere and lively faith, which leads to a godly patience and love for profoundly broken people like me and which has taught me about the character of God.

I am grateful for Christ Presbyterian Church (that is, all of the *people* who make up that sweet congregation), who first corporately spoke these words of confession with me. At Christ Pres. I learned that confession can and should lead to vibrant, sincere, and musical joy, and that confessing to God *together* has a huge impact on everyday relationships. I also owe the Christ Pres. music team a great debt for joining me in my first attempts to explore the importance of connecting confession to song (King David really knew what he was doing when he wrote Psalm 51).

I also want to thank my siblings, Karen and Larissa, and Jamie, Sam, Hannah, Rob, and Rosie. You guys have the undesirable front-row seats (the splash-zone!) to the living examples of the necessity of confession in my life. You have not only seen, but also been on the receiving end of the angry, rude, distracted, overly sensitive, proud, and all-around ungodly and unloving words and actions that I still need to confess so often. Likewise, my dear friends Josh S., Will K., Laura and Joel A., Amy and Chris C., Lauren and Chad W., Winston and Kim S., Will R., Todd S., Nate H., Michelle G., and Joel B. will all be unsurprised by the confessions in this little book, which come out of real experience of sin and brokenness. But what you all have in common (with so many unnamed friends, family, and coworkers) is the spirit of Christ who loves, forgives, and restores relationships. Thank you for loving me faithfully and being the body of Christ to me.

Finally, I am thankful to God (but not nearly as thankful as I should be) for his pursuing, eternal, gracious, life-changing, and relationship-altering love in Jesus. It's his sacrifice that has made these confessions possible and forgiveness guaranteed.

WAYNE DUGUID HOUK

CAPTIVATED BY SIN

✥ CALL TO CONFESSION: GENESIS 3:6–7

So when the woman saw that the tree was good for food, and that it was a delight to the eyes, and that the tree was to be desired to make one wise, she took of its fruit and ate, and she also gave some to her husband who was with her, and he ate. Then the eyes of both were opened, and they knew that they were naked. And they sewed fig leaves together and made themselves loincloths.

✥ PRAYER OF CONFESSION

O God, our Father,

Forgive us for our many sins. Like Eve, we are easily captivated by the objects that our eyes desire. We fall so often, and when we do, we run and hide in shame instead of running to you to confess our sin and find joy and forgiveness in the cross. You have given us your most cherished treasure, yet we prize many other things more highly than Christ. Forgive us for trusting in our own strength more than in his power to save us completely. We live each day with hearts full of our own desires, minds full of our own agendas and plans for our own self-promotion. Forgive us, Lord.

Jesus, you are our strong salvation. Thank you for invading our world to rescue us from ourselves. We cannot fathom the humility, love, and commitment to your Father's glory, which led you to give up heaven for us. When the Holy Spirit took you into the desert to be tempted by Satan, you kept your eyes fixed firmly on your Father, your soul devoted to serving him in perfect obedience, and your mind saturated with Scripture. You gave up your own glory to be stripped, humiliated, and shattered in death, so that you could serve us and be our substitute. The joy of your life was fixed firmly upon the will of God, and now we find the joy of our lives to be your obedience for us and your death in our place. How can we ever thank you adequately?

Holy Spirit, fill us with everlasting wonder that the gospel is true. You kept your promise to send a Savior; help us to stop trying to rescue others and ourselves. When we are tempted to sin as Eve did, remind us of Christ, who kept all your laws for us, and fix our eyes on him. Whether we give in to temptation or resist, show us Christ, our only hope for the perfect obedience that we require to stand before you. Give us the kind of heart that serves you with peaceful abandon, unconcerned about our own welfare and reputation, submissive and quiet before you. Cause us to cherish Christ above all our other desires, so that we will be satisfied in him for all eternity. In his name we pray, amen.

✥ ASSURANCE OF PARDON: JOHN 3:16–17

"For God so loved the world, that he gave his only Son, that whoever believes in him should not perish but have eternal life. For God did not send his Son into the world to condemn the world, but in order that the world might be saved through him."

✥ HYMNS

"All My Heart This Night Rejoices"
"Jesus, Priceless Treasure"

GOD'S PROMISES

✥ CALL TO CONFESSION: GENESIS 17:1–3, 15–17

When Abram was ninety-nine years old the LORD appeared to Abram and said to him, "I am God Almighty; walk before me, and be blameless, that I may make my covenant between me and you, and may multiply you greatly." Then Abram fell on his face. . . .

And God said to Abraham, "As for Sarai your wife, you shall not call her name Sarai, but Sarah shall be her name. I will bless her, and moreover, I will give you a son by her. I will bless her, and she shall become nations; kings of peoples shall come from her." Then Abraham fell on his face and laughed and said to himself, "Shall a child be born to a man who is a hundred years old? Shall Sarah, who is ninety years old, bear a child?"

✥ PRAYER OF CONFESSION

Almighty, infinite Father,

We fall down before you today as glorious saints who love and worship you, and as weak sinners in need of your forgiveness and grace. Like Abraham, we are often far more ready to fall down and laugh at your promises than we are to fall down in awe and wonder at your perfect holiness and astounding love. Your call to walk blamelessly before you weighs heavily on our hearts. Some of us are very aware of just how far short we fall from this command, and we are full of fear and dejected with disappointment in ourselves. Some of us are very blind to our sin and foolishly imagine ourselves to be doing quite well. Lord, thank you that your mercy is more than a match for all our sins of self-hatred and self-righteousness.

As we struggle and fail to live lives of perfect holiness, we thank you for Jesus, who walked blamelessly in our place for thirty-three long years. When Satan tempted him to fall down in worship before him, he chose to obey with absolute faith in you and spotless holiness. With great love and confidence in your promises, he took on all the blame for our disobedience and prideful self-righteousness. By his goodness and death, we are rescued forever from ourselves. Thank you for such a precious redeemer and friend.

Father, fill us with your Holy Spirit and give us faith to believe your promises and live in joyful, confident hope that everything you say is true. When sin threatens to reduce us to despair, show us the covenant love of your Son, crucified for us. Grant us the ability to fall down before the cross each day in confession and repentance, and the grace to shake off our guilty fears and rise with great rejoicing. May the Lord's Supper be a sign and a seal to us of your faithful covenant keeping on our behalf, so that we may be strengthened by it to live as pardoned and reconciled sinners who are dearly cherished by their heavenly Father. Give us growing delight in the blamelessness we have in your wonderful Son, and growing strength to live in holiness and obedience to you. In Jesus' name we pray, amen.

✥ ASSURANCE OF PARDON: GENESIS 17:19, 7; 21:1–3

God said, "No, but Sarah your wife shall bear you a son, and you shall call his name Isaac. I will establish my covenant with him as an everlasting covenant for his offspring after him."

✥✥✥

"And I will establish my covenant between me and you and your offspring after you throughout their generations for an everlasting covenant, to be God to you and to your offspring after you."

✥✥✥

The Lord visited Sarah as he had said, and the Lord did to Sarah as he had promised. And Sarah conceived and bore Abraham a son in his old age at the time of which God had spoken to him. Abraham called the name of his son who was born to him, whom Sarah bore him, Isaac.

✥ HYMNS

"Arise My Soul Arise"
"Poor Sinner Dejected with Fear"
"Thy Mercy, My God"
"Wonderful, Merciful Savior"

LOVING THE WORLD

✣ CALL TO CONFESSION: GENESIS 19:15–16; 1 JOHN 2:15–16

As morning dawned, the angels urged Lot, saying, "Up! Take your wife and your two daughters who are here, lest you be swept away in the punishment of the city." But he lingered. So the men seized him and his wife and his two daughters by the hand, the LORD being merciful to him, and they brought him out and set him outside the city.

✣✣✣

Do not love the world or the things in the world. If anyone loves the world, the love of the Father is not in him. For all that is in the world—the desires of the flesh and the desires of the eyes and pride of life—is not from the Father but is from the world.

✣ PRAYER OF CONFESSION

Merciful Lord,

You have chosen us in Christ to belong to you, set apart from all others in this universe to worship you as our Savior. Left to ourselves, we would still be your enemies, strangers to your love and compassion. Thank you that you have rescued us against our wills. Yet, Father, we continue to sin against you day after day. Like Lot, we are strongly attached to this world and would rather linger and enjoy the sinful delights that it offers than flee from it into your presence and love. We take the best gifts that you offer in creation, and we warp them into instruments of self-worship. We think that we are superior to the people of Sodom and Gomorrah, but you know our hearts and our minds, and we are guilty of these things as well. We devote much of our lives to sexual fantasy and romantic obsession, weaving stories and rehearsing images in our minds that make us feel loved and desirable. When we are not tempted to sin in sexual ways, we feel superior to people who struggle with sexual addictions like pornography and same-sex attraction. Though we can hide these thoughts from others, you know every one of them. Forgive us, we pray.

Father, thank you for giving us a new birth in spite of our sin and rebellion. Lord, part of us longs to be holy and sinless, but there is much in us that still cherishes our sin and clings to it. Please help us to hate our sin and run from it. As you draw us toward heaven, open our eyes and help us to see how offensive our sin is to you, and how damaging it is to us. When we are dazzled by the alluring temptations of sexual and nonsexual sins, teach us that you are the only feast that satisfies our souls deeply and permanently. Fill us with awe and wonder that you give us the radiant robes of your Son's perfection to wear, and carry us to a place of high honor for his glory. Thank you that you have begun a good work in us that nothing can stop, and that one day we will stand before you in the bliss of sinless perfection as Christ's beautiful bride. We give thanks for this in Jesus' name, amen.

✣ ASSURANCE OF PARDON: EPHESIANS 1:3–10

Blessed be the God and Father of our Lord Jesus Christ, who has blessed us in Christ with every spiritual blessing in the heavenly places, even as he chose us in him before the foundation of the world, that we should be holy and blameless before him. In love he predestined us for adoption as sons through Jesus Christ, according to the purpose of his will, to the praise of his glorious grace, with which he has blessed us in the Beloved. In him we have redemption through his blood, the forgiveness of our trespasses, according to the riches of his grace, which he lavished upon us, in all wisdom and insight making known to us the mystery of his will, according to his purpose, which he set forth in Christ as a plan for the fullness of time, to unite all things in him, things in heaven and things on earth.

✣ HYMNS

"Alas, and Did My Savior Bleed"
"Carried to the Table"
"Grace Unmeasured"

GOD'S GOOD GIFTS

✥ CALL TO CONFESSION: GENESIS 22:1–3

After these things God tested Abraham and said to him, "Abraham!" And he said, "Here am I." He said, "Take your son, your only son Isaac, whom you love, and go to the land of Moriah, and offer him there as a burnt offering on one of the mountains of which I shall tell you." So Abraham rose early in the morning, saddled his donkey, and took two of his young men with him, and his son Isaac. And he cut the wood for the burnt offering and arose and went to the place of which God had told him.

✥ PRAYER OF CONFESSION

Lord God Almighty,

You graciously and generously fill our lives with many wonderful things. You bless us with friends, family, and wealth that most people in this world can't even imagine. We confess today that we are prone to love your good gifts far more than we love you. We covet and long for things that you haven't given us, or we are filled with fearful anxiety if we think that you might take away the things or people that we have come to love so much. Father, thank you for your deep and endless mercy to rebels like us. We have trampled on the blood of your precious and only Son, time and time again. We know that we deserve your wrath, and yet when we approach you we find grace and mercy instead. Father, we cannot fathom the cost to your heart of pouring out so much anger on your perfect Son. Father, we are so grateful that you were willing to suffer so much for us.

Jesus, thank you that you have disarmed the wrath of God toward us. You never bowed to an idol or loved anything or anyone more than your Father. You offered perfect worship on our behalf, and by your obedience we are made spotlessly clean. Thank you for walking up the hill of sacrifice for us, for carrying the very wood to which you would be nailed, knowing full well that for you there would be no substitute. Thank you for enduring for us the full fury of your Father's just hatred for sin, and for paying the price for every single idolatrous thought, sinful act, and moment of unbelief we would engage in.

Holy Spirit, help us to see our many idols, and incline our stubborn hearts to repent. Open our blind eyes to see the Lamb of God lifted up for us, so that his redeeming blood could cleanse us from all our self-worship. Draw our eyes to the great throne room in heaven, where he dwells in radiant glory, crowned with honor and interceding for those united to him. Thank you for the certain hope that one day we will join with the thousands upon thousands of the redeemed, falling down before the throne and saying together, "Worthy is the Lamb who was slain, to receive blessing and honor and glory forever." Amen.

ASSURANCE OF PARDON: JAMES 1:16–18; LUKE 11:13

Do not be deceived, my beloved brothers. Every good gift and every perfect gift is from above, coming down from the Father of lights with whom there is no variation or shadow due to change. Of his own will he brought us forth by the word of truth, that we should be a kind of firstfruits of his creatures.

"If you then, who are evil, know how to give good gifts to your children, how much more will the heavenly Father give the Holy Spirit to those who ask him!"

HYMNS

"Behold the Lamb"
"Depth of Mercy"
"Lamb of God"

PARENTS AND CHILDREN

✣ CALL TO CONFESSION: EXODUS 20:12; COLOSSIANS 3:21

"Honor your father and your mother, that your days may be long in the land that the LORD your God is giving you."

✣✣✣

Fathers, do not provoke your children, lest they become discouraged.

✣ PRAYER OF CONFESSION

Loving heavenly Father,

We are all rebellious and ungrateful children. Some of us have actively rebelled against our earthly parents, wishing them out of our lives like the prodigal son. We have ignored their wise counsel, thinking that we possess sufficient wisdom in ourselves. Others have passively rebelled like the elder brother, honoring and obeying our parents with our lips, but in our hearts resenting their control over our lives. Some face the difficult challenge of relating to overcontrolling and unwise parents, a task that we have repeatedly failed to do well. Father, forgive us.

Lord, we who are parents have all sinned against our children. We have exasperated them with our selfish demands, inconsistent discipline, and lack of loving concern for their lives. We have used our children to make us look good before others, and resented and punished them when they have failed. We have pressured them to fulfill our own hopes and dreams rather than to pursue your unique purpose for them. Father, forgive us.

Thank you, Father, for your tender, patient care toward all your children. You are kind and merciful, slow to anger, swift to forgive our sinful rebellion. You pursue the prodigal into the far country, and you come out to meet the angry elder brother where he is. You discipline us tenderly and faithfully, bringing into our lives exactly the circumstances that we need in order to know our dependence upon you and to grow in patient endurance and faith.

Jesus, thank you for being the perfect Son that none of us will ever be. You loved and honored your earthly parents, even though you were yourself their Creator. You especially submitted to the will of your heavenly Father, even though it meant enduring intense suffering and drinking the bitter cup of wrath that we deserved.

Holy Spirit, help us to recognize and delight in the enormous privilege of our adoption as sons and daughters of God. Teach us to submit willingly to the fatherly wisdom of God, revealed in your Word. Give us thankful hearts, too, for the gift of our parents, whom you chose for us in your infinite wisdom. Help us to honor and respect them appropriately. Help us in turn to be good parents to our own children, and to become spiritual fathers and mothers in the Lord to those who are younger than us in the faith. Amen.

ASSURANCE OF PARDON: 1 JOHN 3:1–2

See what kind of love the Father has given to us, that we should be called children of God; and so we are. . . . Beloved, we are God's children now, and what we will be has not yet appeared; but we know that when he appears we shall be like him, because we shall see him as he is.

HYMNS

"Day by Day and with Each Passing Moment"
"How Deep the Father's Love"

FORGETTING OUR HOPE

✥ CALL TO CONFESSION: DEUTERONOMY 6:10–12

"When the LORD your God brings you into the land that he swore to your fathers, to Abraham, to Isaac, and to Jacob, to give you—with great and good cities that you did not build, and houses full of all good things that you did not fill, and cisterns that you did not dig, and vineyards and olive trees that you did not plant—and when you eat and are full, then take care lest you forget the LORD, who brought you out of the land of Egypt, out of the house of slavery."

✥ PRAYER OF CONFESSION

Faithful God,

We come to you today as deeply forgetful people. You have been so much better to us than we deserve, faithfully fulfilling your commitment to give us good things in Christ. Yet we quickly forget all the wonderful gifts that you have already given us, and feel angry and bitter when you won't answer our prayers the way in which we want you to. Instead of remembering your deliverance and running to you daily as our shield of refuge, the anchor of our souls, we prefer to remain in bondage to our idols, because we love our sins and it seems too hard to fight against them. We doubt your goodness and power many times each day and resent the race of obedience that you call us to run. Father, forgive us.

Jesus, thank you for remembering the truth faithfully on our behalf. You worshiped your Father daily, with unwavering faith and unshakable hope in his goodness. Cherishing the Father's unchangeable character, you submitted to his perfect wisdom and trusted him completely in all the circumstances of your life, even when it was most painful. You took refuge in him often in your times of need and never turned toward false gods. Now your obedience becomes our strong encouragement to hope in the midst of continuing weakness, and you continue to advocate our cause as our heavenly High Priest. We have no other hope, nor do we need one.

Holy Spirit, we need your power at work in us to stir up our hope. Help us to know and worship our God as he is, the unchangeable, sovereign King, who has sworn by himself to save us in spite of our perverse foolishness. Cause us to know the certainty of God's great love for us, until we are transformed into people who love him deeply, and are able to run the race with strong confidence and joyful hope in Christ. Open our lips to join the heavenly worship service, and help us look forward to the triumphant coming of our heavenly King. Amen.

✥ ASSURANCE OF PARDON: 2 TIMOTHY 2:8–9, 19

Remember Jesus Christ, risen from the dead, the offspring of David, as preached in my gospel, for which I am suffering, bound with chains as a criminal. But the word of God is not bound! . . .

. . . God's firm foundation stands, bearing this seal: "The Lord knows those who are his," and, "Let everyone who names the name of the Lord depart from iniquity."

✥ HYMNS

"Amazing Grace"
"None Other Lamb"

BLESSING

✥ CALL TO CONFESSION: PSALM 1:1–3

Blessed is the man
who walks not in the counsel of the wicked,
nor stands in the way of sinners,
nor sits in the seat of scoffers;
but his delight is in the law of the Lord,
and on his law he meditates day and night.

He is like a tree
planted by streams of water
that yields its fruit in its season,
and its leaf does not wither.
In all that he does, he prospers.

✥ PRAYER OF CONFESSION

O God from whom all blessings flow,

We have sinned times without number just this week and have repeatedly been guilty of searching for blessings in this world apart from you. Instead of delighting in your Word, we have chosen instead to be counseled by the godless wisdom of our culture. When we do read your Word, we are more prone to meditate on our own goodness for having done so than on your amazing love for us in Christ. You have provided a rich feast for our souls in your Word and the Lord's Supper, yet we are careless in our use of those means, bored by your gospel of grace, and more captivated by your gifts than we are by you. When we do cherish your blessings, we are apt to turn them into idols and grasp at them sinfully. O God, our hearts are wild and unruly, and we confess the perversity that governs our souls day after day.

Father, how can we thank you for your perfect Son? He gave up all the blessings of heaven to become sin for us, choosing to be cursed so that we would be richly blessed forever. He entered our world, deeply immersing himself in it without ever being of it, or caught up in the counsel of sinful systems of thought. He enjoyed your many good gifts and blessings, without ever making idols out of them. He found his blessing and joy in you alone, counseled by your Word alone. He has earned your pleasure for us and satisfied your wrath; thank you.

Holy Spirit, we need you to remind us often that we are clothed every moment in the righteousness of Jesus. As we race through each day chasing blessing in sinful ways, stop us often and remind us that you have already given us every spiritual blessing in Christ. May that truth from your Word captivate and delight us afresh as we find ourselves constantly in need of your mercy and forgiveness. Cause us to move toward godly and wise counselors who encourage us to drink often from fountains of living truth. May we bear the fruit of joy and growing obedience as we meditate on the richness of your blessings to us in Christ, in whom fearful sinners are dearly loved and crowned with a glory that they could never earn. Amen.

✥ ASSURANCE OF PARDON: PSALM 32:1–5

Blessed is the one whose transgression is forgiven,
  whose sin is covered.
Blessed is the man against whom the Lord counts
    no iniquity,
  and in whose spirit there is no deceit.

For when I kept silent, my bones wasted away
  through my groaning all day long.
For day and night your hand was heavy upon me;
  my strength was dried up as by the heat of summer.

I acknowledged my sin to you,
  and I did not cover my iniquity;
I said, "I will confess my transgressions to the Lord,"
  and you forgave the iniquity of my sin.

✥ HYMNS

"Always Forgiven"
"Poor Sinner Dejected with Fear"

CHRIST THE KING

✣ CALL TO CONFESSION: PSALM 2:10–12

Now therefore, O kings, be wise;
be warned, O rulers of the earth.
Serve the LORD with fear,
and rejoice with trembling.
Kiss the Son,
lest he be angry, and you perish in the way,
for his wrath is quickly kindled.
Blessed are all who take refuge in him.

✣ PRAYER OF CONFESSION

Father,

We confess with our lips the blessedness of taking refuge in you. However, our lives proclaim a different story. We sing the wonders of your love, but in our hearts we grumble and complain about your perfect law, under whose wise counsel we chafe. We declare that we long for your coming, but in truth we are more wrapped up in the gifts that you give us than we are in you yourself. Instead of rejoicing in the heritage you have given us, and humbly resting in your wisdom in the trials into which you bring us, we are constantly concerned about the present and fearful for the future. Father, forgive us.

Lord Jesus, thank you that you are the King who rules in truth and grace. You are the First and the Last, the Lord of the nations, worthy of the praises of all peoples. Thank you that you bore the curse of Adam's sin and ours, and that through your perfect obedience you bring unbounded blessing to all those who trust in you. Thank you that you rejoiced perfectly in your Father's law and took refuge in him from life's storms. Thank you that you, the Eternal One, took flesh and died for us, and that you are now alive forevermore, ruling over the entire universe.

Holy Spirit, we thank you that you have been poured out on all nations, bringing Jews and Gentiles together in Christ. Give us renewed hearts that delight to serve and worship you. Fill us with such a passion for the gospel that we long to declare the reign of Christ everywhere we go, both here and to the ends of the earth. Enter in to reign as sovereign in our hearts, that all may bow the knee to Jesus and give him the glory he deserves. Amen.

✥ ASSURANCE OF PARDON: REVELATION 1:12–18

Then I turned to see the voice that was speaking to me, and on turning I saw seven golden lampstands, and in the midst of the lampstands one like a son of man, clothed with a long robe and with a golden sash around his chest. The hairs of his head were white, like white wool, like snow. His eyes were like a flame of fire, his feet were like burnished bronze, refined in a furnace, and his voice was like the roar of many waters. In his right hand he held seven stars, from his mouth came a sharp two-edged sword, and his face was like the sun shining in full strength.

When I saw him, I fell at his feet as though dead. But he laid his right hand on me, saying, "Fear not, I am the first and the last, and the living one. I died, and behold I am alive forevermore, and I have the keys of Death and Hades."

✥ HYMNS

"Joy to the World"
"O Come, O Come, Emmanuel"

MERCY, PURITY, AND HUMILITY

✥ CALL TO CONFESSION: PSALM 18:25–27

With the merciful you show yourself merciful;
with the blameless man you show yourself blameless;
with the purified you show yourself pure;
and with the crooked you make yourself seem tortuous.
For you save a humble people,
but the haughty eyes you bring down.

✥ PRAYER OF CONFESSION

Father of mercy,

Hear us for Jesus' sake. We are sinful in our closest walk with you, and it is only by your mercy that we continue to breathe and live. Your grace has given us faith in the cross, by which we are reconciled to you and brought into your great love. Though we stand before you as guilty sinners, you have reckoned us innocent in Christ. Like the unmerciful servant in the parable, we are grateful for your kindness to us, yet we find it difficult to extend that same mercy and kindness to others. Father, forgive us. Thank you that Christ has been merciful to us and for us, so that now we are clothed in his beautiful righteousness.

Father, we are not pure. Our minds are full of self-exalting, angry, and bitter thoughts. Our lips are impure, and we have sinned often with our bodies. Thank you for the purity of your Son that adorns us each day of our lives.

Father, we are not humble. We love to exalt ourselves and enjoy the praise and admiration of those around us. Father, forgive us for our relentless, powerful pride and self-worship. Thank you for the humility of your Son, who became a servant, enduring deep humiliation and pain to rescue arrogant sinners like us. Thank you for giving us his obedience, and counting us humble in him.

Giver of all graces, we look to you to maintain them in us, for it is hard for us to practice what we believe. Strengthen us against temptation, for our hearts are unexhausted fountains of sin, rivers of corruption since our earliest days, flowing out in all our patterns of behavior. You alone can hold back our evil ways, and without your grace to uphold us, we will surely fall. Keep us aware of our weakness and dependence upon you for strength. Let every trial teach us more of your holiness, peace, and love.

Holy Spirit, we cannot grow or persevere in grace unless you work continually in us. Teach us to walk in humble dependence upon you, and may Jesus Christ be exalted in our minds and hearts. Let us see him in all his glory, worshiped by angels and archangels, adored by those he has redeemed, and make us deeply grateful that the mighty Prince of Peace has loved and rescued us. Amen.

✣ ASSURANCE OF PARDON: PHILIPPIANS 2:8–11

And being found in human form, he humbled himself by becoming obedient to the point of death, even death on a cross. Therefore God has highly exalted him and bestowed on him the name that is above every name, so that at the name of Jesus every knee should bow, in heaven and on earth and under the earth, and every tongue confess that Jesus Christ is Lord, to the glory of God the Father.

✣ HYMNS

"From the Depths of Woe"
"The Servant King"
"You Are My All in All"

THE HELPER OF THE HURTING

✥ CALL TO CONFESSION: PSALM 22:23–24

All you offspring of Jacob, glorify him,
and stand in awe of him, all you offspring of Israel!
For he has not despised or abhorred
the affliction of the afflicted,
and he has not hidden his face from him,
but has heard, when he cried to him.

✥ PRAYER OF CONFESSION

King of heaven,

We confess before you the pride, fear, and selfishness that closes our eyes to hurting people around us. Though we share their flesh and blood, we are quick to look away when their suffering and brokenness make us uncomfortable. Instead of looking at them and seeing their great need, we quickly walk away, and turn toward people who make us feel good. Forgive us for the help that we should have offered this week that we did not. Forgive us for the help that we offered for sinful reasons: to feel proud and superior, to purchase friendship, or to put people in our debt. Forgive us for the times when our hearts have been full of resentment and bitterness toward hurting people for needing us, and toward you for asking us to help them. Lord, we cannot obey you with pure hearts and minds. Thank you that in your deep love for us you have not despised and abhorred us in our great affliction, but treasured us and sent your Son to rescue us.

Jesus, you see our great need and are not ashamed of us. We are crippled and afflicted by weakness and sin, but you rushed to rescue us. You took on the weakness of our human bodies and entered our sin-infested world in order to live the life we could not live. Thank you for seeing the needs of those around you, for loving them in their brokenness, and serving them with pure compassion, clean hands, and a pure heart. Thank you for your perfect obedience, which is credited to us, even though we continue to struggle every day with selfish hearts that lack compassion.

Holy Spirit, melt our hard hearts, for we cannot soften them. Cause us to see how we have been rescued by our great Savior, and give us the desire and ability to open our eyes, to look around us, to see people as they are, and to love them deeply from a heart of gratitude and concern. Help us to enter the worlds of others, to celebrate with them, to grieve with them, and to walk alongside them with caring hearts and hands that are ready to help. May we grow into people who love as we have been loved and who serve as we have been served. Amen.

✥ ASSURANCE OF PARDON: PSALMS 40:1–3; 103:11–13

I waited patiently for the Lord;
  he inclined to me and heard my cry.
He drew me up from the pit of destruction,
  out of the miry bog,
and set my feet upon a rock,
  making my steps secure.
He put a new song in my mouth,
  a song of praise to our God.
Many will see and fear,
  and put their trust in the Lord.

✥✥✥

For as high as the heavens are above the earth,
  so great is his steadfast love toward those who fear him;
as far as the east is from the west,
  so far does he remove our transgressions from us.
As a father shows compassion to his children,
  so the Lord shows compassion to those who fear him.

✥ HYMNS

"How Deep the Father's Love"
"I Come by the Blood"
"It Is Well with My Soul"
"Praise, My Soul, the King of Heaven"

STUBBORN BLINDNESS

✥ CALL TO CONFESSION: PSALM 32:8–10

I will instruct you and teach you in the way you should go;
I will counsel you with my eye upon you.
Be not like a horse or a mule, without understanding,
which must be curbed with bit and bridle,
or it will not stay near you.

Many are the sorrows of the wicked,
but steadfast love surrounds the one who trusts in the Lord.

✥ PRAYER OF CONFESSION

O Lord, our God,

Help us and heal us. We are stubborn, blind people who repeatedly and willfully stray away from you. Like children who don't want their parents to hold their hands while walking through a dangerous city, we will not stay near you. In our blindness, even our ability to confess has been distorted. Some of us are emotionally unaffected by the fact that we are helpless sinners without your mercy, indifferent to the cost of our rebellion. We speak words of confession out of principle, out of duty, or out of habit, but rarely out of a deep awareness of our need and helpless state. Others of us are so undone by our habitual falls into sin that we can barely look up to you for help. Lost in the anxiety of our unbelief, we speak words of confession out of fear, out of desperation, out of hopelessness, but seldom out of confidence that you love us and have invited us into the blessedness of repentance and forgiveness.

Yet Christ has recognized our helpless estate, and has shed his own blood for our souls. This blood, that speaks righteousness for us, gives us confidence to confess our failures to you today. Where we have failed to approach you with honest, sincere, and confident words, Christ stands in our place, laying before you his heart in truth and passion, with no sin or mixed motives.

As he hung on the cross, tortured for our iniquities, the sorrows that were rightfully ours were given to him in fullest measure. Your steadfast love surrounds us because your steadfast love was taken away from him. What a precious, atoning, ransoming love!

Loving Father, create in us clean hearts that are truly broken for our remaining struggles with sin yet utterly confident that your love is more than enough to reach the foulest sinner who trusts in you. Give us this trust in great abundance, Lord, as we continue to wrestle through this earthly journey. Help us to sing now with confidence that Jesus truly is our only boast, and when he returns to take his ransomed children home, let us sing anew, "Hallelujah, what a Savior!" Amen.

ASSURANCE OF PARDON: LAMENTATIONS 3:21–23; PSALM 30:11–12

This I call to mind,
  and therefore I have hope:

The steadfast love of the LORD never ceases;
  his mercies never come to an end;
they are new every morning;
  great is your faithfulness.

You have turned for me my mourning into dancing;
  you have loosed my sackcloth
  and clothed me with gladness,
that my glory may sing your praise and not be silent.
  O LORD my God, I will give thanks to you forever!

HYMNS

"All I Have Is Christ"
"Nothing but the Blood"

OUR HOPE

✥ CALL TO CONFESSION: PSALM 33:18–22

Behold, the eye of the Lord is on those who fear him,
  on those who hope in his steadfast love,
that he may deliver their soul from death
  and keep them alive in famine.

Our soul waits for the Lord;
  he is our help and our shield.
For our heart is glad in him,
  because we trust in his holy name.
Let your steadfast love, O Lord, be upon us,
  even as we hope in you.

✥ PRAYER OF CONFESSION

Loving heavenly Father,

Yours is surpassing greatness, unspeakable goodness, and superabundant grace. Your steadfast love greets us each morning, and your faithfulness is our constant companion. Your mercies are fresh each day, flowing toward us in your patient perseverance and loving guidance. We thank you for personal mercies; for a measure of health, the comforts of home, food, and clothing; for those moments of domestic peace and harmony; and for your ongoing protection of ourselves and those whom we love.

Yet we mourn our sin and profound ingratitude to you. We have not put our hope in you, and we have not waited patiently for you to act on our behalf. We have trusted and delighted in your creation rather than in you, and we have looked to our idols to make us glad, complaining bitterly when they have failed us. We have pressured people with the heavy weight of our needs and expectations, and sinned against them when they disappointed us. Father, forgive us for our many sins. We do not deny them or excuse them, but confess that we have broken your holy law and fallen short of keeping your commands.

Thank you that when we fly repenting to your outstretched arms, you will not cast us off, for Jesus brings us near. You will not condemn us, for he died in our place. You will not point out our mountains of sin, for Jesus has leveled them, and his beauty covers all our deformities. Thank you for your wonderful Son, whose unshakable hope in you in the midst of life's worst circumstances has now become our own.

Holy Spirit, help us to turn away from our sin and cling to the cross. May we hide in the wounds of Jesus and find shelter in his side. Cause us to place all our hopes in the powerful blood of our Savior and his perfect righteousness in our place. When life is painful and difficult, and our souls give way to fear and temptation, root us safely once again on our firm foundation, our only hope in life and in death. Let us know afresh the joy of our salvation: Christ has been faithful for us, and so you will always be faithful to us, for you cannot abandon the Son of God, to whom we are inseparably joined. Amen.

✥ ASSURANCE OF PARDON: ROMANS 5:1–6

Therefore, since we have been justified by faith, we have peace with God through our Lord Jesus Christ. Through him we have also obtained access by faith into this grace in which we stand, and we rejoice in hope of the glory of God. Not only that, but we rejoice in our sufferings, knowing that suffering produces endurance, and endurance produces character, and character produces hope, and hope does not put us to shame, because God's love has been poured into our hearts through the Holy Spirit who has been given to us.

For while we were still weak, at the right time Christ died for the ungodly.

✥ HYMNS

"Jesus Be My All"
"My Hope Is Built on Nothing Less"
"None Other Lamb"
"The Steadfast Love of the Lord"

DELIGHT IN THE LORD

✣ CALL TO CONFESSION: PSALM 37:4–8, 39–40

Delight yourself in the LORD,
  and he will give you the desires of your heart.

Commit your way to the LORD;
  trust in him, and he will act.
He will bring forth your righteousness as the light,
  and your justice as the noonday.

Be still before the LORD and wait patiently for him

. . . .

Refrain from anger, and forsake wrath!
  Fret not yourself; it tends only to evil.

. . . .

The salvation of the righteous is from the LORD;
  he is their stronghold in the time of trouble.
The LORD helps and delivers them

. . . .

  because they take refuge in him.

✣ PRAYER OF CONFESSION

Almighty Lord,

We find great delight in your creation and the good things you have given us to enjoy, but we rarely spend time delighting in you. We tend to enjoy you when you give us what we want, but we become anxious, fretful, and angry when life is hard and you seem unwilling to rescue us from uncomfortable or painful circumstances. We spend many days haunted by guilty fears over the sins that we have committed, forgetting the wounds that will forever scar the hands of your Son, and that plead forgiveness for us every moment of every day. We fail to bear grief and shame patiently, because we forget that you alone are our stronghold in times of trouble, and you are working all things together for our good. Father, forgive us.

We thank you for your radiant and beautiful Son, who delighted in you above all else and perfectly committed all his ways to your sovereign will. We praise you that his flawless obedience is ours through faith, and we are forever reconciled to you as your beloved children. Instead of trying to escape discomfort, Jesus chose the pathway of excruciating pain in order to purchase us. In the tomb he waited patiently for you, trusting in you for his salvation. You delivered him from death, making a showcase of his righteousness and your justice, investing him with great honor and glory. He took refuge in you, and you exalted his name above every other name. Thank you for uniting us to Christ and for loving us in the very same way that you love him.

Father, cause us to find overwhelming delight in the salvation you have given us through Christ. Stir our weak souls to arise and shake off the fearful guilt we cling to with stubborn pride. Open our eyes more and more to see our great High Priest, crushed for us, and now pleading for us before your throne. May we treasure his love and believe with all our hearts that nothing can separate us from it, not even the sin with which we continue to struggle. Give us such great confidence in the gospel that we run joyfully to you in the midst of our weakness, to hear your pardoning voice and feel the ardent and passionate embrace of our true Father. Amen.

ASSURANCE OF PARDON: HEBREWS 10:19–23

Therefore, brothers, since we have confidence to enter the holy places by the blood of Jesus, by the new and living way that he opened for us through the curtain, that is, through his flesh, and since we have a great priest over the house of God, let us draw near with a true heart in full assurance of faith, with our hearts sprinkled clean from an evil conscience and our bodies washed with pure water. Let us hold fast the confession of our hope without wavering, for he who promised is faithful.

✥ HYMNS

"Arise My Soul Arise"
"Be Still, My Soul"

GOD'S FAITHFULNESS

✥ CALL TO CONFESSION: PSALM 40:8–10

"I delight to do your will, O my God;
  your law is within my heart."

I have told the glad news of deliverance
  in the great congregation;
behold, I have not restrained my lips,
  as you know, O LORD.
I have not hidden your deliverance within my heart;
  I have spoken of your faithfulness and your salvation;
I have not concealed your steadfast love and your faithfulness
  from the great congregation.

✥ PRAYER OF CONFESSION

Our great God,

Before you we are full of vanity and iniquity. Our sin has forfeited your favor and corrupted your image, exposing us to the curse of your wrath. Though your law is written deeply on our hearts and consciences, we take little delight in it. You have delivered us from our sin, and continue to deliver us from our foolish weakness, but we are slow to proclaim your faithfulness and speak of your salvation to one another. When you rescue us from pits of destruction, we look on our sin lightly and take your grace and steadfast love for granted. Father, forgive us.

Jesus, you are the Lamb for sinners wounded, and the Rock of our salvation. You withstood the heavy load of our guilt and delivered us from the penalty that we so richly deserved. You did not conceal the glory of your Father, but wrapped yourself in our flesh so that we could see and touch that glory and learn of his steadfast love and faithfulness. You proclaimed God's salvation and deliverance with your lips, your life, your death, and your resurrection. Now, through the gift of faith, your obedience has become our own. Jesus, thank you for your faithfulness to us.

Holy Spirit, we cannot deliver ourselves from our indwelling sin. Help us to find in Jesus the power of our salvation: his death is the center of all relief; his life is the source of all our hope and righteousness. Transform us, by your mercy and grace, into children who are more thankful for your kindness, more humble under your correction, more watchful against temptation, more eager to serve you. Give us hearts overflowing with joy in you and lips that boast often of Jesus Christ, our only hope in life and in death. Rescue us each day from the pit of our own self-sufficiency. May we look to Christ, our Rock and Redeemer, in times of sorrow and of peace, until the day when faith becomes sight and all is well with our souls. Amen.

ASSURANCE OF PARDON: PSALM 40:11, 17

As for you, O LORD, you will not restrain
  your mercy from me;
your steadfast love and your faithfulness will
  ever preserve me!
. . . .
As for me, I am poor and needy,
  but the Lord takes thought for me.
You are my help and my deliverer.

HYMNS

"It Is Well with My Soul"
"Stricken, Smitten, and Afflicted"

BE STILL

✥ CALL TO CONFESSION: PSALM 46:10–11

"Be still, and know that I am God.
I will be exalted among the nations,
I will be exalted in the earth!"
The LORD of hosts is with us;
the God of Jacob is our fortress.

✥ PRAYER OF CONFESSION

Father of mercies,

Quiet our anxious thoughts and help us to be still before you. We confess that we do not run to you as our refuge and strength, but turn to many other sources of hope and help when our souls are troubled. When our lives fall apart and our hearts are like roaring and foaming seas, we are prone to fear you, accuse you, hate you, and feel abandoned by you. If we have been obedient to you, we think that you owe us better than this cup of suffering. When we have disobeyed, we fear that you are judging us and imagine that we have spoiled your wonderful plan for our lives. Father, thank you for your presence with us in our joy and our sorrow, in our strength and our weakness. We praise you that we cannot ruin your plans, for you work all things, even our own sin and the sins of others against us, together for our good and for your glory.

Lord Jesus, you obeyed your Father with every thought and action, yet his wonderful plan for your life was to give you the bitter cup of suffering that should have been ours. You trusted and loved God even when he didn't let that cup pass from you; your faith never wavered when he turned his back on you, so that he would never have to forsake us. Thank you for obeying in our place and giving us your righteousness.

Holy Spirit, exalt Christ in our hearts. Give us strength to trust in him, for we are weak and it is hard to practice what we believe. You alone can restrain our sin, for without your grace to sustain us, we quickly fall. When we resist sin, show us that all the glory is yours and not ours. When we fall, remind us of the oceans of love and forgiveness that are ours in Christ, and of your complete sovereignty over all sin. May we treasure Christ in our weakness and failure, celebrating the love of such a wonderful Savior. Thank you for times of pain when you dismantle our idolatries and disarm the fortresses that we turn to instead of you. When life is stormy, let us find safety, peace, and hope in Christ, our best refuge and only source of true and lasting strength. In his priceless name we pray, amen.

ASSURANCE OF PARDON: PSALM 46:4–5; REVELATION 22:1–5, 20

There is a river whose streams make glad the city of God,
  the holy habitation of the Most High.
God is in the midst of her; she shall not be moved;
  God will help her when morning dawns.

Then the angel showed me the river of the water of life, bright as crystal, flowing from the throne of God and of the Lamb through the middle of the street of the city. . . . No longer will there be anything accursed, but the throne of God and of the Lamb will be in it, and his servants will worship him. They will see his face, and his name will be on their foreheads. And night will be no more. They will need no light of lamp or sun, for the Lord God will be their light, and they will reign forever and ever. . . . Amen. Come, Lord Jesus!

HYMNS

"Be Still, My Soul"
"Come, Thou Fount of Every Blessing"
"Jesus, Priceless Treasure"

THE WILDERNESS OF SIN

✥ CALL TO CONFESSION: PSALM 78:19–22

They spoke against God, saying,
"Can God spread a table in the wilderness?
He struck the rock so that water gushed out
and streams overflowed.
Can he also give bread
or provide meat for his people?"

Therefore, when the LORD heard, he was full of wrath;
a fire was kindled against Jacob;
his anger rose against Israel,
because they did not believe in God
and did not trust his saving power.

✥ PRAYER OF CONFESSION

Heavenly Father,

Thank you for taking us into the wilderness time and time again, for there we see revealed the secret sins of our souls. In the desert we experience your great power to save us from our unruly and sinful hearts, and there we complain bitterly when you withhold the pleasures and delicacies of life we have come to expect. Father, forgive us.

Precious Lord, you have given us your own body as a feast for our salvation and strength. When our spirits are dry and barren, you welcome us to your banqueting table and call us to drink deeply from the overflowing fountain of your goodness and grace. Jesus, thank you for the saving power of your death in our place, and for your spotless obedience, which defeats the vast record of our offenses against you. Because of your death and resurrection, we can know for certain that every desert into which you call us will become a sweet banquet of your wisdom and love, for you do all things for the good of those who love you and are called according to your purpose.

Holy Spirit, help us to trust in Christ so that we can live by faith and not by sight. When you show us the wilderness of our sin, give us grace to repent quickly. Grant us the humility to look away from our failures to celebrate the righteousness that has been given to us. Help us to grow stronger as we try to obey you, and to endure our remaining weaknesses until the day when we kneel before your throne to worship you in heaven. Teach us to wait for that day when we will no longer hunger or thirst, when all our diseases will be healed and every tear will be wiped away. Fill us with hope and joy in you as we pass through the remaining wildernesses that you have ordained for us here on earth. Remind us that Christ has walked through the valley of death for us, and that he will surely walk through each of our valleys with us until we arrive safely in the land of promise that you have prepared for us. Amen.

✣ ASSURANCE OF PARDON: REVELATION 7:13–17

Then one of the elders addressed me, saying, "Who are these, clothed in white robes, and from where have they come?" I said to him, "Sir, you know." And he said to me, "These are the ones coming out of the great tribulation. They have washed their robes and made them white in the blood of the Lamb.

"Therefore they are before the throne of God,
and serve him day and night in his temple;
and he who sits on the throne will shelter them with his presence.
They shall hunger no more, neither thirst anymore;
the sun shall not strike them,
nor any scorching heat.
For the Lamb in the midst of the throne will be their shepherd,
and he will guide them to springs of living water,
and God will wipe away every tear from their eyes."

✣ HYMNS

"Jesus Be My All"
"The Lord's My Shepherd"

SEEKING TRUE BLESSING

✥ CALL TO CONFESSION: PSALM 84:11–12

For the Lord God is a sun and shield;
the Lord bestows favor and honor.
No good thing does he withhold
from those who walk uprightly.
O Lord of hosts,
blessed is the one who trusts in you!

✥ PRAYER OF CONFESSION

Lord God,

We thank you from the depths of our hearts for your wondrous grace and love to us in Christ. You have proven your faithfulness to us in the death and resurrection of your only Son and have promised us that you will not withhold any good thing from us. You are our sun and shield, and we should love to dwell in your presence more than anything else on earth. Yet we confess that we are full of sin and cannot walk uprightly. We are quick to grasp whatever blessings we can for ourselves and reluctant to trust in your perfect will. We scheme endlessly and impatiently to establish our own kingdoms and fail repeatedly to submit to your wisdom, power, and holy will. We have deceived and manipulated others to get our way. Help us to repent of these sins and make us willing to make restitution.

Jesus Christ, without your perfect obedience given to us, we would have no hope at all of receiving favor from our heavenly Father. You walked uprightly on our behalf, yet you were treated like a wretched criminal, losing all honor and favor before your Father, so that we could live forever as treasured sons and daughters of the King. Now you are glorified and exalted, and you have lifted us up and covered our shame with your glory, even though we remain very sinful. Jesus, thank you.

Spirit of the living God, you indwell us and always have your way with us. Help us to find our peace and refuge in God's protection, so that we stop trying so hard to protect ourselves. May we find our true blessing in him, so that we can stop our restless and sinful attempts to grasp blessings for ourselves. Let us rejoice at the end of each day that you have done all things well and have not withheld from us one thing that we needed. Please give us the sweet grace of repentance so we can know your forgiveness, and give us the courage of confession and restitution, since we have been so lavishly loved by our Savior. Thank you for the weakness that keeps us near the cross, marveling at your rich and overwhelming grace to broken sinners. In Christ's name we pray, amen.

✥ ASSURANCE OF PARDON: ROMANS 8:28–32

And we know that for those who love God all things work together for good, for those who are called according to his purpose. For those whom he foreknew he also predestined to be conformed to the image of his Son, in order that he might be the firstborn among many brothers. And those whom he predestined he also called, and those whom he called he also justified, and those whom he justified he also glorified.

What then shall we say to these things? If God is for us, who can be against us? He who did not spare his own Son but gave him up for us all, how will he not also with him graciously give us all things?

✥ HYMNS

"Jesus Be My All"
"Jesus Paid It All"

COVENANT FAITHFULNESS

✣ CALL TO CONFESSION: PSALM 89:24–32

"My faithfulness and my steadfast love shall be with him,
and in my name shall his horn be exalted.
I will set his hand on the sea
and his right hand on the rivers.
He shall cry to me, 'You are my Father,
my God, and the Rock of my salvation.'
And I will make him the firstborn,
the highest of the kings of the earth.
My steadfast love I will keep for him forever,
and my covenant will stand firm for him.
I will establish his offspring forever
and his throne as the days of the heavens.
If his children forsake my law
and do not walk according to my rules,
if they violate my statutes
and do not keep my commandments,
then I will punish their transgression with the rod
and their iniquity with stripes."

✣ PRAYER OF CONFESSION

Faithful heavenly Father,

You are a covenant-keeping God, but we have forsaken your law and violated your statutes. We have not walked according to your rules or kept your commandments. Though you have always been faithful to us, we are unfaithful to you many times each day in our thoughts and with our words and actions. We know that we deserve to be punished for our sin. We have earned the rod of your anger and violent stripes of bitter anguish for our mountains of iniquity. Father, because of your steadfast love, forgive us we pray.

Jesus, you have been faithful in all things for us, keeping covenant with your Father on our behalf. You were the sinless Servant who kept the law perfectly, the perfect Son who walked according to your Father's commandments, and now you have become the Rock of our salvation. You truly earned the steadfast love and faithfulness of God, but willingly surrendered to the punishment that we deserve for all our rebellion. Instead of a throne here on earth, you chose a cross; instead of the honor of a high king, you chose the humiliation of whips and lashes, your flesh torn as you endured our stripes of anguish. You freely took our place, enduring our shame as you were lifted up to die. Thank you, Lord Jesus. Now the empty tomb proclaims God's faithfulness to you, his obedient Son, and to all of us who are united to you. By faith we behold you, the Holy Lamb of God, crowned with glory and honor and seated on a throne that will last forever. You are so worthy to be praised.

Holy Spirit, in our great weakness help us to believe that guilty and vile sinners like ourselves become spotlessly clean in the redeeming blood of Christ. Cause us to see him as our precious jewel, the one great treasure that we seek above all else. Grant us overwhelming joy in this Man of Sorrows who made full atonement for us, and help us to believe and enjoy the truth that it is truly finished. Make us steadfast and faithful until that wonderful day when we see our glorious King and we are brought safely home where we will sing, "Hallelujah, what a Savior," forevermore. Amen.

✥ ASSURANCE OF PARDON: PSALM 89:30–37, 52; HEBREWS 6:17–20

"If his children forsake my law
  and do not walk according to my rules,
if they violate my statutes
  and do not keep my commandments,
then I will punish their transgression with the rod
  and their iniquity with stripes,
but I will not remove from him my steadfast love
  or be false to my faithfulness.

I will not violate my covenant
  or alter the word that went forth from my lips.
Once for all I have sworn by my holiness;
  I will not lie to David.
His offspring shall endure forever,
  his throne as long as the sun before me.
Like the moon it shall be established forever,
  a faithful witness in the skies."

. . . .

Blessed be the LORD forever!
  Amen and Amen.

So when God desired to show more convincingly to the heirs of the promise the unchangeable character of his purpose, he guaranteed it with an oath, so that by two unchangeable things, in which it is impossible for God to lie, we who have fled for refuge might have strong encouragement to hold fast to the hope set before us. We have this as a sure and steadfast anchor of the soul, a hope that enters into the inner place behind the curtain, where Jesus has gone as a forerunner on our behalf.

HYMNS

"Behold the Lamb"
"Man of Sorrows, What a Name!"
"You Are My All in All"

BUILDING OUR OWN HOUSES

✣ CALL TO CONFESSION: PSALM 127:1–2

Unless the Lord builds the house,
those who build it labor in vain.
Unless the Lord watches over the city,
the watchman stays awake in vain.
It is in vain that you rise up early
and go late to rest,
eating the bread of anxious toil;
for he gives to his beloved sleep.

✣ PRAYER OF CONFESSION

Mighty God,

You rule with power and wisdom over the entire universe, and yet you delight in us. We are dependent on you entirely for all things; wean us from all our other dependences. You are the fountain of goodness; why should we be so anxious about what will happen to us? In the light of your favor, the world and all its pleasures are infinitely poor, yet we continue to be drawn to them in so many sinful ways. Forgive us for relying on our own wisdom and strength; for the hours we spend trying to rescue ourselves from pain, suffering, and sin, when you have already rescued us in your Son. Forgive us for frantically building our own lives day after day, when you have called us to rest in you, and for choosing to sin over and over again to advance our agendas, instead of speaking the truth and trusting you to deliver us from the losses that we fear we cannot survive. Heavenly Father, our minds and hearts are full of the sins of self-reliant pride; forgive us.

Wonderful Savior, you have rescued us from ourselves by your perfect obedience in our place. You never sinned to accomplish your will, but obeyed your Father with every thought and action. You have rescued us by taking our punishment, and by dying our death. Now we are raised to new life with you, we are dressed in your glorious perfection, and we are undone by your great and powerful love for very willful sinners like us.

Holy Spirit, comfort us in our weakness by showing us Christ. Make it our chief pleasure to study him, gaze at him, delight in him, trust him, rest in his arms, and follow him. May his finished work for us become more real and enticing than the busy, self-focused work that fills our moments and our days. Give us purposeful energy to set about the tasks you have given us to do, always mindful that without you we can do nothing, and with you we will do all the good works that you have ordained for us. At the end of each day, let us rest in you, knowing that you have accomplished all your holy will for that day in our lives, and that you have done all things well. In Jesus' name we pray, amen.

ASSURANCE OF PARDON: PSALM 103:8–14

The LORD is merciful and gracious,
slow to anger and abounding in steadfast love.
He will not always chide,
nor will he keep his anger forever.
He does not deal with us according to our sins,
nor repay us according to our iniquities.
For as high as the heavens are above the earth,
so great is his steadfast love toward those who fear him;
as far as the east is from the west,
so far does he remove our transgressions from us.
As a father shows compassion to his children,
so the LORD shows compassion to those who fear him.
For he knows our frame;
he remembers that we are dust.

HYMNS

"From the Depths of Woe"
"How Deep the Father's Love"

SUFFERING

✣ CALL TO CONFESSION: PSALM 130:1–3

Out of the depths I cry to you, O Lord!
  O Lord, hear my voice!
Let your ears be attentive
  to the voice of my pleas for mercy!

If you, O Lord, should mark iniquities,
  O Lord, who could stand?

✣ PRAYER OF CONFESSION

All-seeing God,

We confess our sinful response to the trials and discomforts of our lives. While in the depths of woe, we have resented our need for you and rarely lifted our eyes to you, the only one who can bring us true help. Instead we have consistently directed our gaze to earthly things that falsely promise escape and comfort. We have been charmed by vain things: the approval of others; the possessions that we have or want; the allure of misused sexuality; and the enormous drive to worship our bodies, our abilities, and our desires above all things. In our willful blindness to the love and comfort you offer us, we are found completely guilty in your holy sight.

Yet as we continually stray from your love and your law, you look upon our helpless state and lead us to the cross. We ask you to do this now, Father. Thank you that Jesus looked perfectly to you in every single situation of his life, trusting you completely in all things. We are deeply grateful that Jesus never stopped trusting you, even when you did not allow the cup of condemnation that we deserve to pass from him. Jesus had to be lifted up on the cross because of our unwillingness to lift up our eyes to you. Yet Christ's life and death on our behalf is the very comfort to which we are habitually so unwilling to look. Forgive us, Father, for our rejection of this beautiful gospel story into which you have invited us.

Loving God, soften our hearts to delight in your love for us. Change us into sons and daughters who are so enraptured with the story of the gospel that we run to our beautiful Savior as we experience suffering in our lives. Help us to trust you as you call us into journeys that we do not want to take, knowing that you will never leave us or forsake us. Give us strength to believe that from your own fullness you will repay all that you take from us. Lift our eyes afresh to the cross, from whence our help comes, the place where our lives were saved by Jesus' death. In his name we come, amen.

✣ ASSURANCE OF PARDON: PSALM 130:4–6

But with you there is forgiveness,
  that you may be feared.

I wait for the Lord, my soul waits,
  and in his word I hope;
my soul waits for the Lord
  more than watchmen for the morning,
  more than watchmen for the morning.

✣ HYMNS

"All I Have Is Christ"
"Be Still, My Soul"
"Blessed Assurance"
"From the Depths of Woe"
"When I Survey the Wondrous Cross"

PATIENCE

✥ CALL TO CONFESSION: PSALM 130:3–8

If you, O LORD, should mark iniquities,
O Lord, who could stand?
But with you there is forgiveness,
that you may be feared.

I wait for the LORD, my soul waits,
and in his word I hope;
my soul waits for the Lord
more than watchmen for the morning,
more than watchmen for the morning.

O Israel, hope in the LORD!
For with the LORD there is steadfast love,
and with him is plentiful redemption.
And he will redeem Israel
from all his iniquities.

✥ PRAYER OF CONFESSION

Mighty God,

You are the great Creator who made all things from nothing. You are holy perfection, and we owe you perfect lives of adoration and praise. O God, if you kept a record of our sins and held us accountable for them, we could never stand before you for a moment, let alone know you, love you, and approach you in our time of need. Father, help us to be amazed today that with you there is steadfast love and plentiful redemption. Fill our lukewarm hearts with deep and lasting gratitude for our perfect redemption in Christ.

We confess that we find it difficult to wait for you, Lord. As we look back on the cross, we know that you are a promise-keeping God who is wiser, kinder, and more loving than we are. You are powerful beyond our imagination, and you always accomplish your will. You have saved us from sin, you are saving us from ourselves, and you have promised us future salvation, but we want our desires satisfied now. We want excellent health and financial security; peaceful relationships and satisfying careers; perfect spouses, children, parents, and friends; perfect churches; and freedom from weakness and besetting sins. We want heaven now, and we struggle with anger and bitterness when you keep your promise that our lives here on earth will be characterized by suffering and tribulation. We rush frantically from one painful moment to the next, desperately trying to fix our problems and escape discomfort, instead of quieting our hearts before you. Father, forgive us.

Jesus, you waited patiently for your Father's timing. No one hurried you and nothing panicked you, for you trusted your very life to the will of God. From your first breath to your last, you kept the law for us so that we could be freed from its curse. You have been patient for us; now be patient with us and help us to grow into people who put their hope in you and wait for you more than watchmen for the morning. When the time is right you will come again and make all things new. Help us to wait submissively for the fullness of our salvation, and to celebrate joyfully the salvation that you give us every day. Amen.

ASSURANCE OF PARDON: MICAH 7:18–19

Who is a God like you, pardoning iniquity
  and passing over transgression
  for the remnant of his inheritance?
He does not retain his anger forever,
  because he delights in steadfast love.
He will again have compassion on us;
  he will tread our iniquities underfoot.
You will cast all our sins
  into the depths of the sea.

HYMNS

"No, Not Despairingly"
"Out of the Depths"

HOPE IN GOD

✣ CALL TO CONFESSION: PSALM 131

O Lord, my heart is not lifted up;
  my eyes are not raised too high;
I do not occupy myself with things
  too great and too marvelous for me.
But I have calmed and quieted my soul,
  like a weaned child with its mother;
  like a weaned child is my soul within me.

O Israel, hope in the Lord
  from this time forth and forevermore.

✣ PRAYER OF CONFESSION

Loving heavenly Father,

You alone are the Creator and Sustainer of all things. It is our great privilege to live under your omnipotence, righteousness, wisdom, mercy, and grace. You love us with better love than any we could ever know here on earth, and we stand in awe of your power and commitment to cherish us. Yet even though we have tasted your goodness, we are people who would rather trust in ourselves. We place our hope in our own talents and abilities, in relationships with people we admire and love, in our jobs and good health, in our economic value and academic abilities. We even place our hope in spiritual disciplines, thinking that we will merit more favor from you if we deny ourselves, pray constantly, or sacrifice for you and for others. Father, we are worshipers of ourselves, and we find our hearts full of anxiety and depression when we discover that we cannot save ourselves in any way.

Jesus, if you had not lived a perfect life for us, we could never have hope or peace. You trusted your Father throughout your lifetime and into your undeserved death. Thank you for suffering the many agonies of life in a fallen world on our behalf, and for remaining faithful and obedient in temptation, grief, and loss. Your glowing obedience and perfect righteousness are the strong foundation for all our hope and peace. We marvel that you would consider us a joy worth suffering for, and we bow humbly before you and offer you our praise, our thanks, and our very lives.

Holy Spirit, teach us to be still and know that you are God and we are not. Please give us true grief for the many ways we sin against you, and fill us with repentance and hope in you. Open our blinded eyes to see clearly your faithfulness and power; your great love and unending patience; your relentless determination to pursue us, captivate us, and ravish us with the truth of the gospel. Show us the unstoppable love of our Savior, who was stricken for our sin, and who stands in heaven as our powerful Advocate. Then we will be at peace because you are perfect and strong, and you will never leave us, forsake us, or hurt us. Amen.

ASSURANCE OF PARDON: 1 PETER 1:3–8

Blessed be the God and Father of our Lord Jesus Christ! According to his great mercy, he has caused us to be born again to a living hope through the resurrection of Jesus Christ from the dead, to an inheritance that is imperishable, undefiled, and unfading, kept in heaven for you, who by God's power are being guarded through faith for a salvation ready to be revealed in the last time. In this you rejoice, though now for a little while, if necessary, you have been grieved by various trials, so that the tested genuineness of your faith—more precious than gold that perishes though it is tested by fire—may be found to result in praise and glory and honor at the revelation of Jesus Christ. Though you have not seen him, you love him. Though you do not now see him, you believe in him and rejoice with joy that is inexpressible and filled with glory.

HYMNS

"Grace Unmeasured"
"None Other Lamb"

TRUSTING IN MEN

✥ CALL TO CONFESSION: PSALM 146:3–5

Put not your trust in princes,
in a son of man, in whom there is no salvation.
When his breath departs, he returns to the earth;
on that very day his plans perish.

Blessed is he whose help is the God of Jacob,
whose hope is in the LORD his God.

✥ PRAYER OF CONFESSION

Sovereign Commander of the universe,

You are our fortress, our refuge, and our shield. Fight for us, and our foes must flee; uphold us and we cannot fall; strengthen us and we stand unmovable; stand by us and Satan must depart. Anoint our lips with a song of salvation, and we will shout your victory and sing of your triumph.

Father, though you wrap us in the protection of your powerful and loving arms, we frequently turn away from you and put our trust in ourselves and others. We are easily enthralled by human glory and fail to see your glory, wisdom, kindness, and care. We are easily impressed by the strengths of others, putting too much faith in them or envying them, according to our inclinations. We have high expectations of people around us and feel undone when they fail us and behave like ordinary, depraved sinners. Father, forgive us for putting our trust in men and women, and failing to trust you, our King of Glory.

Lord Jesus, your blood and your righteousness soar above the mountains of our sin and plead for us before the throne of grace. Every sinful act of self-worship and man-worship, and the oceans of sin flowing from them, are fully paid for by your atoning blood. Your life of obedience, in which you loved people without ever putting your hope and trust in them, is given to us to replace our own deeply flawed obedience. Jesus, thank you for accomplishing our salvation, and for giving it to us as a free gift.

Holy Spirit, free us from the worship of man, and the fear of man that flows from it. When we idolize and put our trust in others, we cannot love them. Help us to worship God alone, and to know when our hearts are drifting once again into sinful regard for ourselves and others. Open our eyes to see the glory and majesty of our Great King so that we will fly into his loving arms with all our fears, all our cares, and our unbelieving hearts. There may we take refuge in the life and death of our Savior and rest in the power of our victorious King. Teach us to trust and hope in him alone, until the day we stand before him, captivated by his glory, and lost in his love. Amen.

✥ ASSURANCE OF PARDON: PSALM 33:16–22; ROMANS 7:24–25; COLOSSIANS 1:13–14

The king is not saved by his great army;
  a warrior is not delivered by his great strength.
The war horse is a false hope for salvation,
  and by its great might it cannot rescue.

Behold, the eye of the Lord is on those who fear him,
  on those who hope in his steadfast love,
that he may deliver their soul from death
  and keep them alive in famine.

Our soul waits for the Lord;
  he is our help and our shield.
For our heart is glad in him,
  because we trust in his holy name.
Let your steadfast love, O Lord, be upon us,
  even as we hope in you.

✥✥✥

Wretched man that I am! Who will deliver me from this body of death? Thanks be to God through Jesus Christ our Lord!

✥✥✥

He has delivered us from the domain of darkness and transferred us to the kingdom of his beloved Son, in whom we have redemption, the forgiveness of sins.

✣ HYMNS

"Guide Me, O Thou Great Jehovah"
"Jesus Be My All"

THE FEAR OF THE LORD

✣ CALL TO CONFESSION: PROVERBS 3:5–7

Trust in the LORD with all your heart,
  and do not lean on your own understanding.
In all your ways acknowledge him,
  and he will make straight your paths.
Be not wise in your own eyes;
  fear the LORD, and turn away from evil.

✣ PRAYER OF CONFESSION

Redeeming God,

We thank you for making us capable of knowing you, and for awakening our souls to desire you. Help us to approach you with reverence and awe; not with presumption or servile fear, but with holy boldness and joyful expectation. We confess to you today that we are prone to love our own wisdom better than yours. In our weakness we forget to think of you, to ask for your help, or to remember how foolish we are. In our pride and rebellion, we spurn your wise commandments and instruction. We confess to you that we find it difficult to trust you, and we fear you in all the wrong ways. You have punished your precious Son in our place and given us spiritual riches beyond imagination, yet we often live as though you love us and bless us when we are good, and as though you are angry and punish us when we sin. Father, help us to believe that there is no wrath left for us, because you have poured it all out on Christ in our place.

O God, melt our hearts. Give us greater faith to believe that Christ has made an end to all our sin: past, present, and future. In our greatest moments of fear and pride, show us our sin and give us sweet repentance. Open our eyes to see our wonderful Savior and fly to him for refuge. Fill us with vibrant gratitude for your Son, who has trusted you fully in our place, and worshiped you with perfect reverence. He committed himself to your will even when you did not let the cup of your wrath pass him by. He did not lean on his understanding but trusted in your wisdom and goodness even as it led him to the cross. Now his faithfulness has become ours and his righteousness our own; how can we ever thank you?

Holy Spirit, remind us often of our weakness until we learn to run to you quickly for grace in our times of need. Humble us and show us the foolishness of our best thoughts so that we will trust you instead of ourselves. Give us strong desires to love and obey you, and strength to walk in growing obedience. Replace our guilty fear with joyful, awestruck wonder until the good works to which you have called us begin to flow from transformed hearts. Amen.

✣ ASSURANCE OF PARDON: PSALM 23

The LORD is my shepherd; I shall not want.
  He makes me lie down in green pastures.
He leads me beside still waters.
  He restores my soul.
He leads me in paths of righteousness
  for his name's sake.

Even though I walk through the valley of the shadow of death,
  I will fear no evil,
for you are with me;
  your rod and your staff,
  they comfort me.

You prepare a table before me
  in the presence of my enemies;
you anoint my head with oil;
  my cup overflows.
Surely goodness and mercy shall follow me
  all the days of my life,
and I shall dwell in the house of the LORD
  forever.

✣ HYMNS

"Jesus, My Only Hope"
"Revelation Song"

WISDOM

✣ CALL TO CONFESSION: PROVERBS 9:9–10

Give instruction to a wise man, and he will be still wiser;
teach a righteous man, and he will increase in learning.
The fear of the Lord is the beginning of wisdom,
and the knowledge of the Holy One is insight.

✣ PRAYER OF CONFESSION

Lord of all wisdom,

We thank you for the wisdom by which you made this world. You order all nature and history by your wisdom, working all things according to your holy will. You order our personal lives by your wisdom, bringing into them exactly the right combination of joys and sorrows, trials and blessings, to shape us after the image of your beloved Son.

Lord, we confess that we deeply lack wisdom. We have not feared you, but instead have feared people and circumstances, giving the reverence and awe to the created order that belongs to you as our Creator. We have rejected your perfect wisdom, revealed in your Word, preferring to trust the wisdom of this world instead. We have sought to define for ourselves what is good and what is evil in our relationships, our speech, our work, and our sexuality. We have failed to love others as we ought; instead we have hurt them with foolish and unkind words, or with cold and heartless silence. We have grumbled about your providence and the circumstances of our lives, instead of recognizing and delighting in your fatherly wisdom that does all things well.

Jesus, thank you that you are the wisdom of God. Living among us as a man, you reverenced your heavenly Father perfectly. You always obeyed his wise Word, and knew perfectly how to respond to every situation and in every relationship. You gave gentle answers when they were appropriate, spoke convicting words when necessary, and held your peace when that was the wisest response. You never complained about your Father's will for your life, even though it meant learning obedience through suffering. In the end, you paid the penalty that our sinful folly deserved, so that through the wisdom of the cross you might accomplish the Father's plan to redeem your people.

Spirit of wisdom, teach us to seek after wisdom passionately. Wisdom is your gift; give us hearts that desire it and pursue it. Show us how wisdom always leads us back to the cross, on to obedience, and upward toward our heavenly home. Hasten the day when we will join the crowd around the throne in heaven, lost in reverence before the God of all wisdom, the Lamb slain for our sins. Amen.

ASSURANCE OF PARDON: 1 CORINTHIANS 1:27–30

God chose what is foolish in the world to shame the wise; God chose what is weak in the world to shame the strong; God chose what is low and despised in the world, even things that are not, to bring to nothing things that are, so that no human being might boast in the presence of God. And because of him you are in Christ Jesus, who became to us wisdom from God, righteousness and sanctification and redemption.

HYMNS

"A Debtor to Mercy"
"Poor Sinner Dejected with Fear"

CLEANSING FROM SIN

✥ CALL TO CONFESSION: ISAIAH 1:16–17

"Wash yourselves; make yourselves clean;
remove the evil of your deeds from before my eyes;
cease to do evil,
learn to do good;
seek justice,
correct oppression;
bring justice to the fatherless,
plead the widow's cause."

✥ PRAYER OF CONFESSION

Holy God,

We are people who cannot wash ourselves or make ourselves clean. Even as your children, we love evil and resist what you have said is good. We demand justice for ourselves, but fail to pursue it vigorously on behalf of others. We are indignant about the oppression we read of in faraway lands, yet blind to the oppression taking place right here before our eyes in our families, homes, and work places. We feel good when we give money to feed orphans in foreign countries, but we often don't know or care about the widows and orphans who need your love right around us. Father, forgive us.

Redeeming God, we praise you that you have washed us clean in the blood of your Son. You placed all our evil on him so that it could be removed from your sight forever. Jesus suffered profound injustice for our lukewarm apathy, and was fatally oppressed for our continuing failure to love and help the oppressed, here and abroad. He became fatherless to pay for our careless disregard for the fatherless and widows in our own towns. We crucified your precious Son, and instead of hating us, you have given us his perfect goodness and welcomed us to your feast. We are left undone by your extravagant love and complete salvation.

We ask you to wash our minds and hearts clean, moment by moment. Make our hearts good so that works of kindness and mercy flow from us to the needy people you have placed in our lives. May we love them as you have loved us in our great need. Cause us to love justice and, like your Son, to suffer joyfully great injustice on behalf of others. Help us to love extravagantly, as we have been loved by you. Amen.

✥ ASSURANCE OF PARDON: ISAIAH 1:18; 1 CORINTHIANS 6:9–11

"Come now, let us reason together, says the LORD:
though your sins are like scarlet,
  they shall be as white as snow;
though they are red like crimson,
  they shall become like wool."

✥✥✥

Do you not know that the unrighteous will not inherit the kingdom of God? Do not be deceived: neither the sexually immoral, nor idolaters, nor adulterers, nor men who practice homosexuality, nor thieves, nor the greedy, nor drunkards, nor revilers, nor swindlers will inherit the kingdom of God. And such were some of you. But you were washed, you were sanctified, you were justified in the name of the Lord Jesus Christ and by the Spirit of our God.

✥ HYMN

"Ah, Holy Jesus"

UNCLEAN LIPS

✥ CALL TO CONFESSION: ISAIAH 6:5

And I said: "Woe is me! For I am lost; for I am a man of unclean lips, and I dwell in the midst of a people of unclean lips; for my eyes have seen the King, the LORD of hosts!"

✥ PRAYER OF CONFESSION

Lord God Almighty,

As we gaze upon your holiness, we are left devastated by our sinfulness. We are lost in the uncleanness of our lips. Unimaginably selfish, utterly prideful, and crushingly unloving words have been spoken freely from these lips. At the same time, we often use our lips to say good things only so that we will be praised by others or so that you will accept us based on our righteousness. We constantly fail to use our lips to say loving or truthful things because we would rather save ourselves the trouble of loving you and others. We live among others who also have unclean lips: we have been mocked, offended, and hated through the lips of others. We confess that we have often responded to these sins with spiteful anger.

Show us our Savior! The prophet cried, "Woe is me!" as his unclean lips were exposed in light of your holiness. We come boldly to you because the woe that we deserve has been entirely poured out on your Son, Jesus Christ. The sacrifice appointed to redeem our shameful lips was none other than the gruesome death of one whose lips were perfectly clean. Jesus' lips spoke love to children, quieted storms, declared forgiveness to sinners, and remained silent before his accusers. When Jesus was angry, his lips remained pure, as his anger was expressed in ways that continued to fulfill your commandment to love you and others before himself. The very lips that spoke, "Father forgive them," that we might be saved, cried out in agony, "Father, why have you forsaken me?" so that we would not be forsaken. We are left in awe at this unfathomable act of love.

Thank you, Father, that the cross stands empty now. Jesus is risen, and you have made us alive in him. Help us, Lord, to speak in light of this gospel news. May we use our lips to speak the same grace and love that have been so richly lavished upon us. When we fail, Lord, help us to remember the words of forgiveness that have been so powerfully guaranteed by the blood of Jesus. Help us to wait patiently for the day when our faith will be sight, the day our lips will finally and purely sing, "Hallelujah, what a Savior!" In Jesus' name, amen.

ASSURANCE OF PARDON: ISAIAH 6:6–7

Then one of the seraphim flew to me, having in his hand a burning coal that he had taken with tongs from the altar. And he touched my mouth and said: "Behold, this has touched your lips; your guilt is taken away, and your sin atoned for."

HYMNS

"Man of Sorrows, What a Name!"
"Stricken, Smitten, and Afflicted"

TRUST

✤ CALL TO CONFESSION: ISAIAH 30:1, 9, 12–13, 15

"Ah, stubborn children," declares the LORD,
  "who carry out a plan, but not mine,
and who make an alliance, but not of my Spirit,
  that they may add sin to sin."

. . . .

For they are a rebellious people,
  lying children,
children unwilling to hear
  the instruction of the LORD.

. . . .

Therefore thus says the Holy One of Israel,
"Because you despise this word
  and trust in oppression and perverseness
  and rely on them,
therefore this iniquity shall be to you
  like a breach in a high wall, bulging out, and about to
    collapse,
  whose breaking comes suddenly, in an instant."

. . . .

For thus said the LORD God, the Holy One of Israel,
"In returning and rest you shall be saved;
  in quietness and in trust shall be your strength."
But you were unwilling.

✤ PRAYER OF CONFESSION

Holy One,

We confess that we are people who do not trust you. We are stubborn and rebellious, habitually unwilling to hear your loving, fatherly instruction. We have repeatedly despised your words, and have even despised your incarnate Word, Jesus Christ, pursuing him to death. We have carried out our own plans for our lives, disregarding your loving plan, or treating it as second best when that plan involves pain or not getting what we want. When we suffer, we lose confidence that you love us, and we experience spiritual amnesia, living as orphans. We have trusted in our desires for physical and emotional comfort, approval from others, health, wealth, success, or intimacy. We have relied on the perverseness of abusing food, drink, sexuality, or other people to bring us peace. We often do not return to you, we frequently do not rest in you, we seldom are quiet before you, and we consistently do not trust you. Please help us in our helplessness, Lord!

Dear Jesus, what a specific, staggering, atoning love you have shown us in the midst of our weakness. On our behalf, you flawlessly trusted your Father. You relied perfectly on his Spirit, and were willing to obey every element of every law, command, and instruction. Your love for us and your trust of your Father caused you to be silent before your false accusers, enduring torturous punishment for sins you did not commit. The sins you were dying for were ours, and we are eternally, deeply grateful for this inconceivable act of love. Because you took on our sin, becoming an orphan as you were abandoned by your Father, we will never be orphans again. Our sins, though like scarlet, are now as white as snow before the judgment seat, washed in the cleansing, healing stream of the blood drawn from your veins.

Help us, our Father, to trust you in the midst of this earthly life. We grow weary, and our strength is small as we fight against the sin in our hearts and in the hearts of others. Help us to find our all in all in no less than Jesus Christ himself. Cause us to live so that others would see that the strength to trust you could never come from us. Help us to sing salvation songs at the midnight of our sufferings. Awaken us to trust you in the midst of this prison of sinful flesh, and remind us that our freedom has fully and finally been bought by the precious blood of Jesus. In his name we pray, amen.

ASSURANCE OF PARDON: ISAIAH 30:18, 29

Therefore the Lord waits to be gracious to you,
and therefore he exalts himself to show mercy to you.

For the LORD is a God of justice;
blessed are all those who wait for him. . . .

You shall have a song as in the night when a holy feast is kept, and gladness of heart, as when one sets out to the sound of the flute to go to the mountain of the LORD, to the Rock of Israel.

HYMNS

"All I Have Is Christ"
"Behold the Lamb"
"What the Lord Has Done in Me"

WORSHIPING THE KING

✣ CALL TO CONFESSION: ISAIAH 45:22–25

"Turn to me and be saved,
   all the ends of the earth!
   For I am God, and there is no other.
By myself I have sworn;
   from my mouth has gone out in righteousness
   a word that shall not return:
'To me every knee shall bow,
   every tongue shall swear allegiance.'

"Only in the LORD, it shall be said of me,
   are righteousness and strength;
to him shall come and be ashamed
   all who were incensed against him.
In the LORD all the offspring of Israel
   shall be justified and shall glory."

✣ PRAYER OF CONFESSION

Heavenly Father and King,

We come to you today as people who would rather govern our own lives than submit to your rule and shepherding. Instead of bowing down in reverence, full of awe and wonder that you, the almighty creator King of the universe should stoop so low to love and care for us, we often treat you as a servant who should do our bidding and meet all our desires. Instead of honoring the wonderful and merciful Father that you are to us, we run from your goodness and love toward the false and dangerous hopes of our desires and idolatries. Our inability to discipline our wandering ways results in incredible brokenness in our lives and relationships: our families, friends, and coworkers have often become the recipients as well as the source of our sin and pain.

Jesus, thank you for worshiping your Father with unwavering faith and unshakable hope on our behalf. Fully knowing and cherishing his true character, you submitted to his wisdom and trusted him completely in all the circumstances of your life. You ran to him often in your times of need and never turned toward false gods. The brokenness that entered this holy family was not the result of self-promotion or idolatry, but came from the willing sacrifice you made to be separated from your Father in an eternal payment for our sin. Now your obedience is ours, and we are so grateful to be united to you and defined by your righteousness instead of our own.

Holy Spirit, we are utterly feeble and weak, and we need your power at work in us. Help us to know and worship our God as he is, our King and Father who loves us passionately in the middle of our perverse foolishness. Press the truth of your gospel deep into our souls so that we see the work of our triune God: the Father, the radiant Potentate of time, and the lover of our souls; Jesus, the Man of Sorrows, humble, weary, bleeding for us, but at the same time the glorious Lamb upon the throne, crowned with many crowns, and worshiped by angelic hosts; and the Holy Spirit, the Lord and Giver of life, who is graciously at work in our hearts and lives. Cause us to know and feel God's great love for us until we are transformed into people who love others deeply because of a great sense of our own need and an undeniable sense of our forgiveness and adoption. Open our lips to join the heavenly worship service and sing praises to our heavenly King, today, tomorrow, and forevermore. Amen.

ASSURANCE OF PARDON: PSALM 138:1–8

I give you thanks, O Lord, with my whole heart;
  before the gods I sing your praise;
I bow down toward your holy temple
  and give thanks to your name for your steadfast love
    and your faithfulness,
  for you have exalted above all things
  your name and your word.

On the day I called, you answered me;
  my strength of soul you increased.

All the kings of the earth shall give you thanks,
    O Lord,
  for they have heard the words of your mouth,
and they shall sing of the ways of the Lord,
  for great is the glory of the Lord.
For though the Lord is high, he regards the lowly,
  but the haughty he knows from afar.

Though I walk in the midst of trouble,
  you preserve my life;
you stretch out your hand against the wrath of my enemies,
  and your right hand delivers me.
The Lord will fulfill his purpose for me;
  your steadfast love, O Lord, endures forever.
  Do not forsake the work of your hands.

HYMNS

"Crown Him with Many Crowns"
"Jesus Be My All"
"Jesus, Lover of My Soul"
"Wonderful, Merciful Savior"

FORGETTING GOD

✤ CALL TO CONFESSION: ISAIAH 51:7–8

"Listen to me, you who know righteousness,
 the people in whose heart is my law;
fear not the reproach of man,
 nor be dismayed at their revilings.
For the moth will eat them up like a garment,
 and the worm will eat them like wool;
but my righteousness will be forever,
 and my salvation to all generations."

✤ PRAYER OF CONFESSION

Ransoming Lord,

We confess that we do not listen to you or remember who you are. We are quick to forget that you stretched out the heavens and laid the foundations of the earth with a word. You created us and everyone around us, and you alone are from everlasting to everlasting. You are the one who judges all men in righteousness and truth. Because we often forget this truth, we fear and worship people instead of you, and give them the power to cast us into despair by their judgments of us. Instead of trusting and rejoicing in your verdict of "not guilty," we are undone by their displeasure and devastated by their criticism. Sometimes they revile us for our actions and we are crushed, even though we have not broken your law, but only the laws of men. At other times, when they reproach us for truly breaking your law, we hear only their words of condemnation and not the comforting words of the gospel. When we love your righteousness and feel your law written on our hearts, we have trouble remembering your grace and forgiveness. Forgive us, Lord.

We thank you, Lord, for the perfect goodness of your Son, who knew and loved your law with all his heart, mind, soul, and strength, in our place. He never feared the reproach or criticism of men, nor was dismayed at their reviling. Instead he spoke the truth in love at all times, fearlessly serving others instead of worshiping them. Yet on the cross he paid the deadly price for all our fear-driven adoration of the approval of men. His body was slain and bathed in blood as he withstood your fearful wrath for all our crimes. His loving hands were pierced with nails, his faithful head bloodied with thorns, as he listened to the mocking ridicule of those he came to save. He cried out in anguish, so that we would never know the anguish of trying to pay for our own sin.

Father, we desperately need your help to know your righteousness in all its fullness, and to love your law well. Cause us to see the glory of your Son, Jesus Christ, so that we remember your grace as well as your justice. Dissolve our hearts in thankfulness by reminding us of the cross many times each day and drawing our hearts to be amazed by your outrageous love for us. Wean us from our addiction to glory and the admiration of others by persuading us of the truth that you delight in us every moment of every day. You love us exactly as much as you love your Son, Jesus, because we are forever joined to him. May this truth melt our eyes to tears and fill us with unfathomable joy. Amen.

ASSURANCE OF PARDON: ISAIAH 51:11, 14–16

The ransomed of the LORD shall return
  and come to Zion with singing;
everlasting joy shall be upon their heads;
  they shall obtain gladness and joy,
  and sorrow and sighing shall flee away.

. . . .

"He who is bowed down shall speedily be released;
  he shall not die and go down to the pit,
  neither shall his bread be lacking.
I am the LORD your God,
  who stirs up the sea so that its waves roar—
  the LORD of hosts is his name.
And I have put my words in your mouth
  and covered you in the shadow of my hand,

establishing the heavens
and laying the foundations of the earth,
and saying to Zion, 'You are my people.'"

✥ HYMNS

"Alas, and Did My Savior Bleed"
"I Am the Lord Your God"

WANDERING

✥ CALL TO CONFESSION: ISAIAH 53:4, 6

Surely he has borne our griefs
  and carried our sorrows;
yet we esteemed him stricken,
  smitten by God, and afflicted.
. . . .
All we like sheep have gone astray;
  we have turned—every one—to his own way;
and the LORD has laid on him
  the iniquity of us all.

✥ PRAYER OF CONFESSION

O God, our Savior,

We come before you today as foolish sheep who find it our natural inclination to wander far from you. You have set your love upon us, chosen us, and saved us, but we find it hard to trust you and prefer to turn to our own wisdom and understanding. You lead us in green pastures for your own name's sake, but we reject the feast that you lay before us and try frantically to fill ourselves up with things that cannot satisfy. You lead us by still waters to restore our souls, yet we recklessly dabble with strong currents of temptation and are easily swept away by torrents of sinful cravings and lust. You call us to straight paths of righteousness, but we scorn your warnings, ignore your guidance, and rebel against your discipline. You have given us the great privilege of knowing and worshiping our Creator, the one true God, but we prefer to bow before our worthless idols day after day in search of the morsels of comfort or pleasure they offer to us. Father, we stray from you every day and turn to our own ways; forgive us for our many sins.

Jesus, you are our sacrificial lamb. You never strayed from the path of obedience to your Father, even when that path led you to a brutal cross and the mockery of those who should have worshiped and adored you. As a sheep before its shearers is dumb, you refused to argue against the charges made against you, for you knew you would become sin for us, taking on the guilt of those belonging to you. Jesus, you are the Great Shepherd, who laid down your life for your beloved, silly sheep, and you are the tender shepherd who gathers us in your arms and carries us. Thank you for refusing to turn to the path of your own glory, so that we could be safely gathered into your fold. You were torn for all our sinful and rebellious wandering, and through your wounds we find healing and peace. Thank you.

Holy Spirit, help us to see where the path of blessing lies, and give us hearts that are eager to travel that path. While we live in a fallen world with sinful hearts, we will always be prone to wander. Thank you for holding fast to us, for we cannot hold onto you. Give us strong appetites for spiritual food: the Word of God and the body and blood of our precious Savior. Grant us unshakable confidence in the death and life of Jesus, until his wounds cleanse our guilt and give us great joy. Make us humble followers instead of prideful leaders, so that we can find safety and delight in walking with you. In Jesus' name we pray, amen.

✣ ASSURANCE OF PARDON: ISAIAH 53:5

But he was pierced for our transgressions;
he was crushed for our iniquities;
upon him was the chastisement that brought us peace,
and with his wounds we are healed.

✣ HYMNS

"He Was Wounded for Our Transgressions"
"His Forever"
"The Lord's My Shepherd"

THE BEATITUDES

✥ CALL TO CONFESSION: MATTHEW 5:3–12

"Blessed are the poor in spirit, for theirs is the kingdom of heaven.

"Blessed are those who mourn, for they shall be comforted.

"Blessed are the meek, for they shall inherit the earth.

"Blessed are those who hunger and thirst for righteousness, for they shall be satisfied.

"Blessed are the merciful, for they shall receive mercy.

"Blessed are the pure in heart, for they shall see God.

"Blessed are the peacemakers, for they shall be called sons of God.

"Blessed are those who are persecuted for righteousness' sake, for theirs is the kingdom of heaven.

"Blessed are you when others revile you and persecute you and utter all kinds of evil against you falsely on my account. Rejoice and be glad, for your reward is great in heaven, for so they persecuted the prophets who were before you."

✥ PRAYER OF CONFESSION

Blessed Lord God,

Your Word searches our hearts and condemns us. We are not poor in spirit: we are proud and self-dependent. We do not mourn over our sin and the sin of others: we hide and excuse our sin, while judging others for their sin. We are not meek but are eager to defend our own rights and reputations, while caring little for your good name and the name of others. We hunger and thirst far more to get our own way than for your righteousness. We easily forget the mercy that we have received, and as a result feel little mercy toward others. Our hearts are not pure but are divided between serving you and serving our idols. We have jealous thoughts that promote strife in our words and actions, instead of loving and pursuing your peace. We flee from the smallest hint of persecution, eagerly protecting our own comfort and security, instead of boldly proclaiming your truth like the prophets. Lord God, we confess before you that we deserve your eternal curse for all these things.

Thank you, Father, for Jesus Christ, in whom we are blessed with every spiritual blessing. His dependence, mourning, meekness, hunger for righteousness, mercy, purity, peacemaking, and faithfulness even to death are the righteousness that enables us to receive your blessing. Because of his obedience, our reward is great in heaven.

Lord, teach us to live as those who are blessed in Christ. Help us to proclaim to others the mercy we have received and to live lives that are in line with that mercy and holiness. Help us to love the righteousness that redeemed us and to long for the day when you will work that righteousness in fullness in our hearts. Purify our hearts and cleanse our minds increasingly, so that we may endure hardship as good soldiers for Jesus Christ, and may delight to bear the burdens of those whom you place around us. Amen.

ASSURANCE OF PARDON: PSALM 32:1–5

Blessed is the one whose transgression is forgiven,
 whose sin is covered.
Blessed is the man against whom the LORD counts no
  iniquity,
 and in whose spirit there is no deceit.

For when I kept silent, my bones wasted away
 through my groaning all day long.
For day and night your hand was heavy upon me;
 my strength was dried up as by the heat of summer.

I acknowledged my sin to you,
 and I did not cover my iniquity;
I said, "I will confess my transgressions to the LORD,"
 and you forgave the iniquity of my sin.

HYMNS

"Come Ye Sinners"
"Poor Sinner Dejected with Fear"

ANGER

✥ CALL TO CONFESSION: MATTHEW 5:21–22

"You have heard that it was said to those of old, 'You shall not murder; and whoever murders will be liable to judgment.' But I say to you that everyone who is angry with his brother will be liable to judgment; whoever insults his brother will be liable to the council; and whoever says, 'You fool!' will be liable to the hell of fire."

✥ PRAYER OF CONFESSION

Holy Lord,

We have sinned against you deeply and profoundly. For some of us, that sin has taken the form of outward acts of rage and violence. Others of us may not have sinned outwardly in these ways, yet we have carefully tended and protected in our hearts the root from which such sins grow. We may not have murdered anyone, but our hearts are a cesspool of violent feelings against those who frustrate us and cross our wills. We have nurtured angry and bitter thoughts against others because they did not treat us with the respect that we thought that we deserved or give us the glory that we sought. Some of us have used harsh words to wound people, while others have used passive silence as a weapon of abuse. Some of us have simply concealed our true feelings behind a cloak of deception, isolating ourselves from those around us.

Forgive us for our unrighteous and self-serving anger, Lord. Help us to see the root from which it springs—the desire that we should ourselves be as God and have others bow to us and do our will. Lord, fill us with wonder as we see how the true God deals with hardened rebels against his will. You are the one who has a right to have a holy anger toward us for our rebellion. Yet you poured out your holy rage upon Christ in our place, exposing him to the awful curse of the cross. It was our sinful anger and malicious hate that brought him there, and yet he freely sacrificed his own life for the sake of our reconciliation to you.

Lord, teach us to put off our anger and replace it with loving self-sacrifice. Teach us to prefer to be wronged than to spit back angry words; teach us to set aside our interests and preferences and to put the welfare of others ahead of our own desires; teach us to long for your glory more than for our own, and thus to share as ambassadors in your ministry of reconciliation to this lost and dying world. Amen.

✣ ASSURANCE OF PARDON: 2 CORINTHIANS 5:17–18, 21

If anyone is in Christ, he is a new creation. The old has passed away; behold, the new has come. All this is from God, who through Christ reconciled us to himself. . . . For our sake he made him to be sin who knew no sin, so that in him we might become the righteousness of God.

✣ HYMNS

"From the Depths of Woe"
"Jesus Paid It All"
"Out of My Bondage, Sorrow and Night"

SEXUALITY

✣ CALL TO CONFESSION: MATTHEW 5:27–28

"You have heard that it was said, 'You shall not commit adultery.' But I say to you that everyone who looks at a woman with lustful intent has already committed adultery with her in his heart."

✣ PRAYER OF CONFESSION

Lord God of heaven,

We confess before you the ways in which we have abused your gift of sexuality. You gave us sex to be a wonderfully good gift within marriage, but we have perverted it in so many ways, using it to distract us from our boredom or loneliness, or to make us feel loved and accepted. We have used our sexuality as a means to serve our idols, instead of receiving it as a gift from you, to be used as you intended.

There is not one of us who is blameless in your sight in this area. Some of us confess before you physical acts of impurity that have left us feeling defiled and dirty. Others have committed the same acts in our minds and are thus equally guilty before you. Some have used our sexuality to manipulate others and gain their attention, or have created a romantic fantasy world in which others exist to worship us. Some are self-righteously proud of what we have not done, using our purity as grounds for boasting before you, when any vestige of purity that we have is a gift from you.

Heavenly Father, we acknowledge that sexual brokenness is only one small window into the pervasive brokenness of our lives as your image bearers. Thank you for Jesus' perfect obedience in this area, as in every other, which enables us to stand before you forgiven and cleansed in him. Lord, help us to take our sexual brokenness to the cross; help us to experience the comfort and peace that comes to us in the gospel and that enables us increasingly to say no to our idols. Teach us how to reach out to others for help and to support one another in our struggles and failures. Give us grace in our marriages to delight in our sexuality as a way of serving and enjoying one another. Above all, may our brokenness fill us with still deeper longing for the day when we will finally be made whole, when Jesus Christ returns. Amen.

✣ ASSURANCE OF PARDON: JEREMIAH 3:20, 22–23; MATTHEW 9:10–12

"Surely, as a treacherous wife leaves her husband,
so have you been treacherous to me, O house of Israel,
declares the LORD."

. . . .

"Return, O faithless sons;
I will heal your faithlessness."
"Behold, we come to you,
for you are the LORD our God.

. . . .

Truly in the LORD our God
is the salvation of Israel."

✣✣✣

As Jesus reclined at table in the house, behold, many tax collectors and sinners came and were reclining with Jesus and his disciples. And when the Pharisees saw this, they said to his disciples, "Why does your teacher eat with tax collectors and sinners?" But when he heard it, he said, "Those who are well have no need of a physician, but those who are sick."

✣ HYMNS

"All I Have Is Christ"
"More Love to Thee"

LYING

✣ CALL TO CONFESSION: MATTHEW 5:33–37

"You have heard that it was said to those of old, 'You shall not swear falsely, but shall perform to the Lord what you have sworn.' But I say to you, Do not take an oath at all, either by heaven, for it is the throne of God, or by the earth, for it is his footstool, or by Jerusalem, for it is the city of the Great King. And do not take an oath by your head, for you cannot make one hair white or black. Let what you say be simply 'Yes' or 'No'; anything more than this comes from evil."

✣ PRAYER OF CONFESSION

Heavenly Father,

We confess the times that we have not promoted truth in this world. Forgive us for being a people whose hearts are so deceitful that we even deceive ourselves. We say one thing and do another, making promises but not fulfilling them. We lie outright to others, or we mislead them for our own selfish gain. We say whatever it takes so that we can get what we want. Indeed we are most like the Devil himself when we deceive, for he is the Father of Lies.

At times we speak falsely against others, and in so doing hurt their good reputation. At other times we refuse to give proper credit to those who deserve it. We give unwarranted praise to those we favor, while exaggerating the flaws that we see in our enemies. We hide truth so that we can glorify ourselves, but we ungraciously expose truths that belittle others. When we are honest, we often abuse the truth by not speaking out of love, or by not seeking to use it to help and build up. We also abuse truth when we gossip: sensationalizing the truth to gain popularity.

You alone are true, heavenly Father, and we reveal the depths of our rebellion against you when we rebel against the truth. Grant us forgiveness through your Son, who is the way, the life, and the truth. Thank you for crediting us with the truthfulness of your Son, so that in him we are counted as if we were people who had never told a single lie. Shape us, mold us, and conform us to your truth that we might better reflect your glory. Teach us to be a people who love the truth, and who love to use the truth in a righteous and gracious way, like your Son. Hear our prayer for his sake. Amen.

✥ ASSURANCE OF PARDON: JOHN 1:12–14, 16–17

To all who did receive him, who believed in his name, he gave the right to become children of God, who were born, not of blood nor of the will of the flesh nor of the will of man, but of God.

And the Word became flesh and dwelt among us, and we have seen his glory, glory as of the only Son from the Father, full of grace and truth. . . . From his fullness we have all received, grace upon grace. For the law was given through Moses; grace and truth came through Jesus Christ.

✥ HYMN

"All My Heart This Night Rejoices"

LOVE FOR ENEMIES (1)

✥ CALL TO CONFESSION: MATTHEW 5:43–45

"You have heard that it was said, 'You shall love your neighbor and hate your enemy.' But I say to you, Love your enemies and pray for those who persecute you, so that you may be sons of your Father who is in heaven. For he makes his sun rise on the evil and on the good, and sends rain on the just and on the unjust."

✥ PRAYER OF CONFESSION

O Lover of the unlovely,

It is your will that we should love you with all our heart, soul, mind, and strength, and that we should love our enemies and our neighbors as ourselves. We confess to you that we are not sufficient for these things. By nature, there is no pure love in our souls, and every affection in us is turned away from you and others and toward ourselves. We are prisoners of our own lust and self-worship until you set us free. We fear and despise our enemies, hoping for their ruin and at times causing it. We break covenants with our friends carelessly, and fail to keep the promises we have made. Father, forgive us for our many sins.

Lord, thank you for your perfect Son, who loved his enemies even as he was punished for their sin and tortured in their place. He showed tender love to the most evil and ungrateful people, those who were just like us in every way. When Jesus sought refuge in you as he was dying, you looked away and allowed him to be utterly crushed by the mountain of our sins. He was stripped so that we might be clothed in his righteousness; he was wounded so that we might be healed; he was tormented so that we might be comforted; he was shamed so that we could inherit eternal glory; he entered darkness to be our light; he was made an enemy so that we could be your friends. Thank you for the cross and for our great salvation!

Father, help us to become kind and merciful lovers of our friends and enemies. Open our eyes to your amazing love and generosity toward us until we are transformed into your image, to love as you love. When we are sinned against, cause us to cherish your great mercy to us and then extend it freely to other wretched sinners like ourselves. May we always see ourselves accurately as helpless sinners in need of grace, so that we never move beyond the cross or consider ourselves better than our worst enemies. Thank you for loving us when we hated you, and for abandoning your precious Son to welcome us into your family forever. Amen.

ASSURANCE OF PARDON: ROMANS 5:8–10

God shows his love for us in that while we were still sinners, Christ died for us. Since, therefore, we have now been justified by his blood, much more shall we be saved by him from the wrath of God. For if while we were enemies we were reconciled to God by the death of his Son, much more, now that we are reconciled, shall we be saved by his life.

HYMNS

"Amazing Grace"
"Rock of Ages"

HYPOCRISY

✥ CALL TO CONFESSION: MATTHEW 6:5–8

"And when you pray, you must not be like the hypocrites. For they love to stand and pray in the synagogues and at the street corners, that they may be seen by others. Truly, I say to you, they have received their reward. But when you pray, go into your room and shut the door and pray to your Father who is in secret. And your Father who sees in secret will reward you.

"And when you pray, do not heap up empty phrases as the Gentiles do, for they think that they will be heard for their many words. Do not be like them, for your Father knows what you need before you ask him."

✥ PRAYER OF CONFESSION

Holy God,

We come before you now to confess to you our sin of hypocrisy. Many of us have loved to hear words come out of our mouths, words that often sound profoundly religious. Others of us have retreated into a world of silence in order to cover up the inward turmoil we desperately want to hide. Both of these behaviors come from hearts in need of your grace. We pray that your Spirit would awaken us to our great need for you in this, our sin of self-love.

We have viewed our conversations with others as opportunities to show off our knowledge. Bible studies, classrooms, offices, homes, and even our prayers have become forums in which we love to be seen and heard by others. At other times, we remain sinfully silent when we should be using our words to build up your body and confess to others our weakness and need for you. In both of these situations, we have sought the approval of others, and not of you, committing the greatest offenses against your holy law—we have not loved our neighbors, and we have not loved you.

Savior God, we thank you that you have not left us in this state of sin. We look to the cross, and thank you that Jesus never once uttered a prayer that was not perfect in motivation, intent, or content. His conversations were characterized by love for others, and love for you. Yet for the joy that was set before him, Jesus was crucified for our foul tongues, our love of self, and our hypocrisy. He, the true Word, was put to death for our false words. Lord, thank you for giving us to him, as a gift for this sacrifice, and thank you that in his sacrifice we have been set free from the sin that nailed him to the cross. Thank you too for his continued faithful intercession for us as our heavenly High Priest.

Father God, we ask that you would continually turn our eyes upon the deep love you have displayed to us in Jesus, and that out of gratitude for the amazing grace we see there, our hearts and lives would be changed. Continue to conform us into the image of your Son, so that our relationships would be characterized by love and our prayers be characterized by honesty. Amen.

ASSURANCE OF PARDON: HEBREWS 4:14–16

Since then we have a great high priest who has passed through the heavens, Jesus, the Son of God, let us hold fast our confession. For we do not have a high priest who is unable to sympathize with our weaknesses, but one who in every respect has been tempted as we are, yet without sin. Let us then with confidence draw near to the throne of grace, that we may receive mercy and find grace to help in time of need.

HYMNS

"How Deep the Father's Love"
"More Love to Thee"

FORGIVENESS (1)

✥ CALL TO CONFESSION: MATTHEW 6:9, 12, 14–15

"Pray then like this:

> 'Our Father in heaven,
>
> . . . .
>
> Forgive us our debts,
>   as we also have forgiven our debtors.'
>
> . . . .

"For if you forgive others their trespasses, your heavenly Father will also forgive you, but if you do not forgive others their trespasses, neither will your Father forgive your trespasses."

✥ PRAYER OF CONFESSION

Gracious and forgiving Father,

How often we fail to show the same grace and forgiveness to others that you have given to us! We find it desperately hard to show forgiveness to our spouses and our friends, our parents and our children, our brothers and our sisters. Instead we keep a precise record of the wrongs that they have committed against us; we cherish that record deep in our hearts and use it against them in order to justify ourselves. We hold bitter grudges against others and lash out in revenge at the slightest provocation. We are swift to anger and slow to forgive, whether that anger overflows publicly in boiling rage or simmers quietly in the cold recesses of our hearts.

Yet you are not like us. Even though we have committed far worse sins against you, you do not keep a record of our wrongs; instead you separate our transgressions from us as far as the east is from the west. You deserve perfect obedience from us, for you are a holy and good God, who has loved us profoundly. You planned and worked for our good even when we were your sworn enemies. Even now, whenever we rebel against you, you freely forgive us all our sins, for the sake of Jesus Christ, and you continually work all things together for our good.

Help us today to taste afresh your grace to us in the gospel, and to see anew the depths of our sin that you have forgiven. Transform us by your grace, so that we may become people who readily forgive others, just as you have already forgiven us. May we truly learn to forgive those who sin against us, from the depths of our hearts. We pray in Jesus' name, amen.

✣ ASSURANCE OF PARDON: COLOSSIANS 2:13–14

And you, who were dead in your trespasses and the uncircumcision of your flesh, God made alive together with [Christ], having forgiven us all our trespasses, by canceling the record of debt that stood against us with its legal demands. This he set aside, nailing it to the cross.

✣ HYMNS

"Grace Unmeasured"
"Poor Sinner Dejected with Fear"

FASTING

✣ CALL TO CONFESSION: MATTHEW 6:16–18

"And when you fast, do not look gloomy like the hypocrites, for they disfigure their faces that their fasting may be seen by others. Truly, I say to you, they have received their reward. But when you fast, anoint your head and wash your face, that your fasting may not be seen by others but by your Father who is in secret. And your Father who sees in secret will reward you."

✣ PRAYER OF CONFESSION

Holy Father in heaven,

We confess before you how little we live for your pleasure. Many of us do not fast, because we are primarily concerned about our own comfort and pleasure. We don't mourn over our own sin, or grieve over the profound grip that the world has over us. We don't feel the brokenness of this present world deeply enough to pray with intense passion for you to intervene in it for your glory. We have forgotten the feast that will be laid before us in heaven and have tried to fill our inner hunger with the things of this world.

If we do fast, or when we pursue other spiritual activities such as attending Bible studies or leading in the church, our motivation is often to show off our spirituality to others. We love to be seen as more spiritual than we are, and to be praised as those who are passionately devoted to you. Yet when acts of humble service are to be done, or when no one is watching us, the ugly truth is exposed about who we really are: we are not constantly drawn to pursue your fatherly pleasure. We perform to polish our own self-image or gain praise from others, but do not really seek you.

Thank you that Jesus Christ was not like us. He lived his whole life faithfully pursuing the goal of hearing you declare, "This is my son, with whom I am well pleased." His prayers, actions, and service always came from an undivided heart. Thank you that he was crucified for our hypocrisy and that his single-hearted obedience is now counted as ours.

Show us today the deceptiveness of our own hearts, which constantly pretend to a level of devotion that is not real. Enable us to recognize increasingly how self-serving our religiosity really is. Teach us truly to repent not only for our sin but even for the religious acts we use to try to impress others and gain your favor. Help us to turn our backs on our attempts at righteousness, and instead become people who cling with ever greater passion to the perfect righteousness of Christ in our place. Amen.

✥ ASSURANCE OF PARDON: MATTHEW 11:28–30

"Come to me, all who labor and are heavy laden, and I will give you rest. Take my yoke upon you, and learn from me, for I am gentle and lowly in heart, and you will find rest for your souls. For my yoke is easy, and my burden is light."

✥ HYMNS

"Be Still, My Soul"
"From the Depths of Woe"

TREASURE

✣ CALL TO CONFESSION: MATTHEW 6:19–21

"Do not lay up for yourselves treasures on earth, where moth and rust destroy and where thieves break in and steal, but lay up for yourselves treasures in heaven, where neither moth nor rust destroys and where thieves do not break in and steal. For where your treasure is, there your heart will be also."

✣ PRAYER OF CONFESSION

Lord Jesus,

We confess that we have long been loving treasures that have nothing to do with you or your kingdom. We love material treasures, such as our money, friends, cars, clothes, family, bodies, careers, and talents. We demonstrate that these are our treasures by finding deep satisfaction in them, or by our jealousy of those who have what we do not. We have also sought after the treasure of approval, finding our refuge in our performance, in praise from our employers, friends, and family, thus building our identity on a foundation made of sand. We have even sought to lay up treasures in heaven through our own good behavior, as if your favor could be bought by our efforts.

What a patient Savior you are! We thank you, Jesus, for your perfect obedience on our behalf, constantly seeking first God's kingdom and his glory. You always understood where true treasure lies. When Satan tempted you with the riches of the world, you withstood him. When ridiculed for proclaiming the truth, you remained obediently in communion with your Father. Although you were heir of all things, you set aside this treasure, enduring the poverty of being forsaken by the Father. Though we continue daily to value other things ahead of you, you were put to death so that we, the very ones who crucified you, might become your treasure. For this, we are profoundly grateful.

Help us, Lord Jesus, to respond in faith to this good news. Break in and steal our idol-worshiping hearts. Build our faith on nothing less than you, our refuge and true foundation. Remind us of our utter poverty in ourselves and the riches you have lavished upon us. Turn our hearts from earthly treasure, so that we may rightly treasure you above all else.

✥ ASSURANCE OF PARDON: ISAIAH 55:1–3

"Come, everyone who thirsts,
  come to the waters;
and he who has no money,
  come, buy and eat!
Come, buy wine and milk
  without money and without price.
Why do you spend your money for that which is not bread,
  and your labor for that which does not satisfy?
Listen diligently to me, and eat what is good,
  and delight yourselves in rich food.
Incline your ear, and come to me;
  hear, that your soul may live;
and I will make with you an everlasting covenant,
  my steadfast, sure love for David."

✥ HYMNS

"God, Be Merciful to Me"
"Hide Away in the Love of Jesus"
"Jesus, Priceless Treasure"

EYES

✥ CALL TO CONFESSION: MATTHEW 6:22–23

"The eye is the lamp of the body. So, if your eye is healthy, your whole body will be full of light, but if your eye is bad, your whole body will be full of darkness. If then the light in you is darkness, how great is the darkness!"

✥ PRAYER OF CONFESSION

Holy God,

Our bodies are full of darkness. The lens through which we view the world has been an utterly self-centered one. We have viewed others as objects that exist for our consumption: some of us are haunted by the images we have lusted after: television, Internet, movies, or billboards. But we have brought these fantasies into real time, as well. We have used our eyes to violate those with whom we come in contact on a daily basis. Some of us have demeaned others by haughtily looking down on them for their plain features or lack of style, or else jealously scorning those whom we find to have those attributes we want so badly: thinness, physical strength, or style. Though our individual eyes rest on different objects, this we have in common: our eyes have been drawn easily and often away from you, our creator God.

But amidst this darkness we see a great light. Lord Jesus, you are the Light of the World. When you left your throne to take on human flesh, you literally saw the world with eyes just like ours, yet without sin. You saw people as they truly were, not for what you could get from them. Though tempted in every way as we are, your eyes remained pure and undefiled, leaving your body full of light. Yet it was this body that hung lifeless on the cross due to the darkness of our sin. It was your eyes that were filled with agony as your Father poured upon you the wrath that we deserved.

We are indeed debtors to your mercy! We long to see with new eyes, and ask that you would help us to look away from the images that we have stored up in our minds. Help us to look upon others with love and compassion, remembering that they are made in your image. We long to see you, Jesus. Then we will finally see the Savior who looked upon us with great love, saw us as great treasure, and paid for us at a great price. Amen.

ASSURANCE OF PARDON: LUKE 4:17–21

And the scroll of the prophet Isaiah was given to [Jesus]. He unrolled the scroll and found the place where it was written,

> "The Spirit of the Lord is upon me,
> because he has anointed me
> to proclaim good news to the poor.
> He has sent me to proclaim liberty to the captives
> and recovering of sight to the blind,
> to set at liberty those who are oppressed,
> to proclaim the year of the Lord's favor."

And he rolled up the scroll and gave it back to the attendant and sat down. And the eyes of all in the synagogue were fixed on him. And he began to say to them, "Today this Scripture has been fulfilled in your hearing."

HYMNS

"A Debtor to Mercy"
"In Christ Alone"

CONFLICTING MASTERS

✤ CALL TO CONFESSION: MATTHEW 6:24

"No one can serve two masters, for either he will hate the one and love the other, or he will be devoted to the one and despise the other. You cannot serve God and money."

✤ PRAYER OF CONFESSION

Father God,

You have brought us into your kingdom, but we run from you daily and worship other gods. We love food, sex, our jobs, titles, bodies, good works, possessions, family, and friends more than we love you. We crave approval, power, respect, and comfort, and are willing to sin frequently to get them. In loving these, we tell you that we hate you. By being devoted to our idols, we despise you, and have become enslaved to creation rather than our Creator. We live in bondage to hard taskmasters that leave us feeling empty, alone, and full of shame. Forgive us, Lord, for falling with the first Adam.

Tempted, tried, and often failing, we look now to you for strength. Thank you, Jesus, that your yoke is easy and your burden light. You have taken on the great burden of these sins that we cannot bear. You were tempted by Satan with earthly comfort, glory, and authority, but you trusted and obeyed your Father instead. You endured poverty, shame, and a criminal's death on our behalf. Though we crucified you because of our hatred and spite, you did not despise us. You lovingly saved us, standing in our place as the second Adam.

We are now bound to your grace, our Savior. Free us from all that rules our hearts beside you. Deliver us from slavery to our besetting sins by constantly reminding us of your excellent love for us. Replace our likeness to the first Adam with your likeness, Son of God. Help us to despise the false security, comfort, and pleasure our sins offer, so that we might be devoted to you, in whom we find delight, fulfillment, and true rest. Amen.

✣ ASSURANCE OF PARDON: ROMANS 5:18–19; 1 CORINTHIANS 15:22

Therefore, as one trespass led to condemnation for all men, so one act of righteousness leads to justification and life for all men. For as by the one man's disobedience the many were made sinners, so by the one man's obedience the many will be made righteous.

✣✣✣

For as in Adam all die, so also in Christ shall all be made alive.

✣ HYMNS

"All I Have Is Christ"
"Hark! the Herald Angels Sing"
"Jesus, What a Friend for Sinners"
"More Love to Thee"

ANXIETY

✣ CALL TO CONFESSION: MATTHEW 6:25, 32–34

"Therefore I tell you, do not be anxious about your life, what you will eat or what you will drink, nor about your body, what you will put on. Is not life more than food, and the body more than clothing? . . . For the Gentiles seek after all these things, and your heavenly Father knows that you need them all. But seek first the kingdom of God and his righteousness, and all these things will be added to you.

"Therefore do not be anxious about tomorrow, for tomorrow will be anxious for itself. Sufficient for the day is its own trouble."

✣ PRAYER OF CONFESSION

God of peace,

Forgive us for our anxiety-filled lives. Though our needs have always been met, we fear losing what we already have, and we do not trust you to provide us with money, jobs, spouses, or other things that we need. Many of us are already anxious about tomorrow, with its needs that we do not yet see. We live in constant fear that you do not really care deeply for us, and that our sin will cause you to abandon us. We are daily waiting for the bad news that will confirm our fears: a failed test, a lost job, betrayal by a friend, abandonment by a spouse, rebellion by a child. Instead of seeking first your kingdom and your righteousness, we have fixed our eyes on our own health, safety, comfort, and status.

Yet you showed your deep love for us, Father, by sending your Son to earn your favor in our place. Jesus sought your kingdom and your righteousness above all things, even to the point of dying on the cross for the very sins that we confess today. You poured out your anger against our unbelief and sinfully anxious hearts upon Jesus, so that we might receive a right relationship with you as a gift. You have adopted us as children just as we are—broken, weary, and anxious—because of his righteousness. For this, we are profoundly and eternally grateful.

Lead us, Lord, by the power of your Spirit, to walk in repentance and faith, and to come boldly into your presence by his blood. Help us to seek your kingdom above all things, trusting in Jesus for our righteousness, and believing that you are sovereign over the smallest details of our lives. Remind us, Lord, of the many ways you know and lovingly meet our needs on a daily basis; help us never to forget the eternal inheritance you have prepared for us in Christ that frees us of our fear of the last enemy, death itself. We come in Jesus' name, amen.

✥ ASSURANCE OF PARDON: ISAIAH 43:1–3

Thus says the Lord,
he who created you, O Jacob,
  he who formed you, O Israel:
"Fear not, for I have redeemed you;
  I have called you by name, you are mine.
When you pass through the waters, I will be with you;
  and through the rivers, they shall not overwhelm you;
when you walk through fire you shall not be burned,
  and the flame shall not consume you.
For I am the Lord your God,
  the Holy One of Israel, your Savior."

✥ HYMNS

"And Can It Be"
"Come Ye Sinners"

JUDGING OTHERS

✦ CALL TO CONFESSION: MATTHEW 7:1–5

"Judge not, that you be not judged. For with the judgment you pronounce you will be judged, and with the measure you use it will be measured to you. Why do you see the speck that is in your brother's eye, but do not notice the log that is in your own eye? Or how can you say to your brother, 'Let me take the speck out of your eye,' when there is the log in your own eye? You hypocrite, first take the log out of your own eye, and then you will see clearly to take the speck out of your brother's eye."

✦ PRAYER OF CONFESSION

Father,

We come laden with guilt for our sinfully judgmental attitudes and absurd hypocrisy. There is no end to the list of ways that we judge others. We consider ourselves experts on the things that matter to us, and look at those around us with disdain and disgust as we evaluate their inability to be as intellectual, funny, fashionable, talented, experienced, balanced, reasonable, sensitive, loving, pure, wise, God-fearing, gospel-centered, or generally just as good as we are. Our hypocrisy is shocking as we willfully blind ourselves to the mountain of remaining sin in our own lives while we examine with smug satisfaction the broken and sin-stained lives of those around us. Forgive us, Lord.

We need a Savior! We call upon Jesus' name for deliverance from our love of self and judgment toward others. As Jesus perfectly fulfilled every one of your commands, his attitude toward others remained unshakably characterized by love and compassion. Even as he was being punished for our sinful self-addiction and hypocrisies that we now confess, Jesus was pleading, "Father, forgive them." You poured out your just wrath for our injustices on him. He emptied himself of all but love, so that we in our helplessness would receive adoption by his shed blood.

We are still helpless, Father. Try as we might, we continue to struggle with judgmentalism and hypocrisy, even now. Lead us, Lord, to Calvary, where we see our sin in the blinding light of your love for us through the wonderful cross. Send your Spirit to end the strife in our broken hearts, that we might look at one another with the love and compassion that you have lavished upon us. Let us experience the transforming power of your wonderful grace. In Jesus' powerful name, amen.

✦ ASSURANCE OF PARDON: JOHN 8:3–5, 7, 9–11

The scribes and the Pharisees brought a woman who had been caught in adultery, and placing her in the midst they said to him, "Teacher, this woman has been caught in the act of adultery. Now in the Law Moses commanded us to stone such women. So what do you say?" . . . And as they continued to ask him, he stood up and said to them, "Let him who is without sin among you be the first to throw a stone at her." . . . But when they heard it, they went away one by one, beginning with the older ones, and Jesus was left alone with the woman standing before him. Jesus stood up and said to her, "Woman, where are they? Has no one condemned you?" She said, "No one, Lord." And Jesus said, "Neither do I condemn you; go, and from now on sin no more."

✦ HYMNS

"And Can It Be"
"Laden with Guilt and Full of Fears"

LOVING OTHERS

✥ CALL TO CONFESSION: MATTHEW 7:12

"Whatever you wish that others would do to you, do also to them, for this is the Law and the Prophets."

✥ PRAYER OF CONFESSION

Glorious Father,

We are left uncomfortably exposed by Jesus' words. In the blinding light of your law of love, we stand woefully condemned. If we were treated as we treat others, we would be devastated. We would be despised for our outward appearance, rejected for our sinful behavior, and ridiculed in secret gossip. We would be slighted, cursed, and mocked. We would be misused sexually, abused emotionally, and abandoned relationally. This is precisely what we have done to others, consistently and willingly. Father, forgive us.

Unburden our minds by the atoning work of Jesus, our Redeemer. Remind us that you harbor no wrath toward us, Lord, because you poured out your holy judgment of these sins on Jesus. The powerful voice that spoke only in love and truth toward others cried out in agony as you abandoned him for the sins that we confess this day. The humble voice that pled, "Father, forgive them," was silenced so that we might be free to cry out to you in confidence now. We may come boldly because Jesus did for us what we could never do for ourselves. He fulfilled your law of love by being condemned in our place. We are amazed by this stunning act of grace.

Lord, help us to live in the blessed assurance that we are your adopted children because of what Jesus has done. Fulfill your righteous law of love in us so we might genuinely love and serve one another daily. As we do so, help us to look forward to our heavenly home, where we will see our Savior with new eyes: found by his grace, and lost in his love. Amen.

✥ ASSURANCE OF PARDON: ROMANS 8:1–4

There is therefore now no condemnation for those who are in Christ Jesus. For the law of the Spirit of life has set you free in Christ Jesus from the law of sin and death. For God has done what the law, weakened by the flesh, could not do. By sending his own Son in the likeness of sinful flesh and for sin, he condemned sin in the flesh, in order that the righteous requirement of the law might be fulfilled in us, who walk not according to the flesh but according to the Spirit.

✣ HYMNS

"Blessed Assurance"
"Poor Sinner Dejected with Fear"
"Wonderful Grace of Jesus"

FOLLOWING CHRIST

✥ CALL TO CONFESSION: MATTHEW 8:19–20

And a scribe came up and said to him, "Teacher, I will follow you wherever you go." And Jesus said to him, "Foxes have holes, and birds of the air have nests, but the Son of Man has nowhere to lay his head."

✥ PRAYER OF CONFESSION

Heavenly Father,

You are our great King. We are eager to declare our willingness to go where you command and follow wherever you lead. Yet we confess that we are very weak and fickle. We are easily distracted, constantly diverted from your ways, and quick to follow our own sinful hearts instead. As we plan our futures, we think more of our safety, comfort, and financial profit than we do of laying down our lives for the sake of your kingdom. We are eager to please our families and friends, and slow to consider your calling and your glory our highest goal.

Thank you, Lord Jesus, that you did not guard your own interests, but chose to leave the comfort and richness of heaven for us. When you came to earth, you did not build a secure and comfortable home for yourself, but camped out in the open air or lived in the homes of others. Your first bed on earth was a dirty feeding trough; your last bed, a stone slab in a cold tomb. You made yourself vulnerable, not only to the harsh elements of nature, but also to the foul hatred of those you had come to save. You even gave up the precious fellowship you had shared with your Father from all eternity, to make your rebellious enemies into your redeemed brothers and sisters. Your obedient, joyful self-sacrifice now enables us to stand before our Father, forgiven of our self-centeredness and clothed in your obedience.

Teach us what it means to take up our cross daily and follow you. Help us put to death our overwhelming desires to control our own lives in the present and future. Show us the emptiness of owning nice things, the shallowness of the praise of others, and the offensiveness of our enormous pride. Fill us with such a burning passion for your glory that we will suffer any loss, ridicule, inconvenience, or cost, in order to hear your name praised in every land, from the rising of the sun to the place where it sets. Change our selfish hearts. Enlarge them with a love and gratitude toward you so immense and powerful that following you will be our greatest joy and delight. Amen.

✥ ASSURANCE OF PARDON: 1 CORINTHIANS 1:4–5, 7–9

I give thanks to my God always for you because of the grace of God that was given you in Christ Jesus, that in every way you were enriched in him in all speech and all knowledge . . . so that you are not lacking in any gift, as you wait for the revealing of our Lord Jesus Christ, who will sustain you to the end, guiltless in the day of our Lord Jesus Christ. God is faithful, by whom you were called into the fellowship of his Son, Jesus Christ our Lord.

✥ HYMNS

"Be Thou My Vision"
"God, Be Merciful to Me"
"Jesus, I My Cross Have Taken"

MERCY

✣ CALL TO CONFESSION: MATTHEW 9:12–13

But when [Jesus] heard it, he said, "Those who are well have no need of a physician, but those who are sick. Go and learn what this means, 'I desire mercy, and not sacrifice.' For I came not to call the righteous, but sinners."

✣ PRAYER OF CONFESSION

Compassionate Father,

We confess to you that we don't want to need your mercy. When we see ourselves as righteous before you, we become lovers of ourselves instead of lovers of mercy; we perform to try to impress you instead of showing mercy because we ourselves have been profoundly rescued. Religious duties become more important than loving people, and we easily become blind to the needs of those around us. Sometimes caring for others even becomes the very duty we use to justify ourselves. God, forgive us and have mercy on us.

Father, you have shown us great mercy through the sacrifice of your Son. You piled the awful weight of our sin on Jesus and crushed him in our place, and through his atoning death we have inherited every spiritual blessing imaginable. Dissolve our cool, indifferent hearts with the blazing truth of your astonishing love for us in Christ.

Jesus, you have been merciful to us and for us. You knit yourself to human flesh and walked through this sin-sick world with eyes of love that saw the overwhelming needs of those around you. You loved and cared for people in their suffering, even when they invaded your privacy and disrupted your plans. Serving others was your spiritual duty, so you healed on the Sabbath without confusion or guilt. So now, even though we are confirmed lovers of ourselves and often calloused to the suffering of others, we are credited with all your loving compassion, as though we had done it ourselves. Jesus, how can we ever thank you?

Holy Spirit, keep us mindful of our weakness and sin so that we will come to love the righteousness of Jesus. Melt our stony hearts with gratitude for the mercy we have received until compassion and love flow out of us like a river. Help us to die to our own desires, schedules, agendas, and wisdom, and open our eyes to see the people you want us to love. Give us joyful confidence that you have prepared good works for us to do, and that we will walk in them because you always get your way. Cover our shameful lack of mercy and love for others with the glorious obedience of Jesus, and may our growing love for him compel us to face a needy world with peace and real power to help. Amen.

✣ ASSURANCE OF PARDON: PSALM 103:8–14

The LORD is merciful and gracious,
  slow to anger and abounding in steadfast love.
He will not always chide,
  nor will he keep his anger forever.
He does not deal with us according to our sins,
  nor repay us according to our iniquities.
For as high as the heavens are above the earth,
  so great is his steadfast love toward those who fear him;
as far as the east is from the west,
  so far does he remove our transgressions from us.
As a father shows compassion to his children,
  so the LORD shows compassion to those who fear him.
For he knows our frame;
  he remembers that we are dust.

✣ HYMN

"Depth of Mercy"

COMPASSION

✥ CALL TO CONFESSION: MATTHEW 9:36

When he saw the crowds, he had compassion for them, because they were harassed and helpless, like sheep without a shepherd.

✥ PRAYER OF CONFESSION

Lord,

You are our faithful shepherd who walks beside us in green pastures and through the valley of deep shadow. You have promised to pursue us with your goodness and mercy all the days of our lives. Yet we confess that we often doubt your compassion and care for us. When we are harassed and helpless, instead of turning to you and trusting you to care for our needs and lead us in straight paths, we seek help in our idols and comfort in our sins. When others around us are harassed and helpless, we are impatient and lacking in compassion, uncaring about their needs and concerns. Father, forgive us.

Jesus, thank you for the compassion that brought you from heaven to live among us as the Good Shepherd. Thank you for entering life's trials and enduring death's valley in our place, without fear. Thank you that you always trusted your Father's care for you, even when he gave you the overflowing, bitter cup of suffering to drink for us. Thank you that you have prepared a bounteous feast for us in your Father's house and that we will dwell there in heaven with you forever.

Holy Spirit, be our comforter in the midst of the trials of life. Help us to trust you to provide when we are helpless to do so. Teach us to find refuge in you when we have nowhere else to turn and when no one else seems to understand our needs. Enable us in turn to show similar compassion and care to others as well, we pray, so that we may learn to love the other members of your flock as you do. In Jesus' name, amen.

✥ ASSURANCE OF PARDON: 1 PETER 2:22–25

He committed no sin, neither was deceit found in his mouth. When he was reviled, he did not revile in return; when he suffered, he did not threaten, but continued entrusting himself to him who judges justly. He himself bore our sins in his body on the tree, that we might die to sin and live to righteousness. By his wounds you have been healed. For you were straying like sheep, but have now returned to the Shepherd and Overseer of your souls.

✥ HYMNS

"The Lord's My Shepherd"
"Poor Sinner Dejected with Fear"
"Savior, Like a Shepherd Lead Us"

FORGIVENESS (2)

✥ CALL TO CONFESSION: MATTHEW 18:21–22

Then Peter came up and said to him, "Lord, how often will my brother sin against me, and I forgive him? As many as seven times?" Jesus said to him, "I do not say to you seven times, but seventy-seven times."

✥ PRAYER OF CONFESSION

Merciful Father,

We have often been quick to judge and slow to forgive our brothers and sisters. We notice and keep score for every sin that others commit against us. Sometimes we punish them by lashing out in anger, while at other times we treat them with silent coldness, instead of extending mercy and grace. We have dismissed their attempts at repentance as insincere words, and have held grudges against them, instead of forgiving them freely. At times, we have not even given them the chance to make amends by graciously showing them their sin but have simply assumed that they would be unwilling to repent.

Thank you, Father, that this is not how you have treated us. You have mercifully accepted our flawed repentance, in spite of our divided hearts. You have not held our sin against us, though we have grieved and sinned against you countless times, boldly and brashly, not merely out of ignorance or oversight but with deliberate defiance. Instead you have taken every last one of our sins and crucified them in Jesus, your Son. In place of our failure and sin, you have substituted Christ's perfect obedience and righteousness. Christ's forgiving love pled for the forgiveness of those who were actually crucifying him. We confess that we were the ones who spilt his blood; we have trampled upon your Son. Yet in your grace you see us as having the same forgiving spirit of Christ! We have not been dealt with according to our sins, because Jesus has. We have been given infinite grace by this loving Advocate.

Gracious Lord, help us to worship you in light of these truths. Enable us to love and forgive one another in the same way that you have loved and forgiven us. Teach us to see every sin against us by a brother or sister in Christ as having been nailed to the cross. In place of the record that we keep of one another's wrongs, help us to ponder the record of Christ's righteousness, which is sufficient to pay for our brother's sins, just as it has paid for ours. Help us to become people who, knowing that they have been forgiven much, are themselves deeply forgiving, even toward those who have sinned against us many times. In Jesus' merciful name, amen.

✣ ASSURANCE OF PARDON: 1 JOHN 1:8–9

If we say we have no sin, we deceive ourselves, and the truth is not in us. If we confess our sins, he is faithful and just to forgive us our sins and to cleanse us from all unrighteousness.

✣ HYMN

"Depth of Mercy"

SERVANTHOOD

✥ CALL TO CONFESSION: MATTHEW 20:25–28

But Jesus called them to him and said, "You know that the rulers of the Gentiles lord it over them, and their great ones exercise authority over them. It shall not be so among you. But whoever would be great among you must be your servant, and whoever would be first among you must be your slave, even as the Son of Man came not to be served but to serve, and to give his life as a ransom for many."

✥ PRAYER OF CONFESSION

Loving heavenly Father,

Forgive us for our selfish desire to have others serve us, and for our love of power and influence. You call us to be servants who lovingly pour out our lives for those around us. Lord, our hearts are deceitful, desperately wicked, and relentlessly self-focused. When we do honor, care for, and serve others, we secretly hope that people are watching and noticing so that our humility will be applauded and praised. As a result, our best acts of love toward others are often actually directed toward ourselves, as we use them to impress you and build our résumés before a watching world. Forgive us for our very deep sinfulness.

Precious Savior, you knew that we could never escape our self-love and passion for power and influence. You gave up all power to become weak and helpless. You took on our frail flesh in order to obey and suffer in our place. Thank you for loving weak, poor, helpless, and socially rejected people on our behalf. You are the great Creator of the universe and had every right to exert your power and influence over all of us, yet you came to serve. Thank you for your gentle humility, and for your righteous anger on behalf of those who were oppressed. Thank you for suffering for our prideful, glory-loving hearts, and for giving us your perfect righteousness. Thank you for choosing the cross so that we could be free from the punishment that we deserve.

Holy Spirit, fill our hearts with a deep and burning gratitude for our life in Christ. We have been freed from the power of sin to send us to hell; now free us from our love of power and glory. Wean us from self-love; fill us instead with love for Christ and a desire to serve others as we have been served. Show us our sinful thoughts and motives, then melt our hearts with sweet repentance and show us Christ again and again. May he increase, and may we decrease in our thoughts and desires, until it feels like a privilege simply to do his bidding, and to love and serve those he has called us to care for. Amen.

✥ ASSURANCE OF PARDON: PHILIPPIANS 2:8–11

And being found in human form, [Jesus] humbled himself by becoming obedient to the point of death, even death on a cross. Therefore God has highly exalted him and bestowed on him the name that is above every name, so that at the name of Jesus every knee should bow, in heaven and on earth and under the earth, and every tongue confess that Jesus Christ is Lord, to the glory of God the Father.

✥ HYMNS

"The Servant King"
"What the Lord Has Done in Me"

BEHOLD THE LAMB

✥ CALL TO CONFESSION: MARK 15:17–20; LAMENTATIONS 5:15–16

Twisting together a crown of thorns, they put it on [Jesus]. And they began to salute him, "Hail, King of the Jews!" And they were striking his head with a reed and spitting on him and kneeling down in homage to him. And when they had mocked him, they stripped him of the purple cloak and put his own clothes on him. And they led him out to crucify him.

✥✥✥

The joy of our hearts has ceased;
  our dancing has been turned to mourning.
The crown has fallen from our head;
  woe to us, for we have sinned!

✥ PRAYER OF CONFESSION

King of heaven,

We long to worship you today with hearts full of joy, but we have sinned countless times and we have no crown of glory or obedience to wear before you. Our dancing is turned to mourning when we think of our sin. We understand that we are like the mockers who scoffed at Jesus as he died, the rebels who pressed the crown of thorns deeply onto his sinless head. We are undone and wonder how you could ever love us and welcome us as cherished sons and daughters. Father, forgive us for hearts that doubt you and turn away from you many times each day. Forgive us for worshiping other gods, and then running away in cycles of shame and guilt because we are disappointed in ourselves. Forgive us for believing that our sin is so much stronger than your love and grace.

Lord, thank you for your perfect Son, who never sinned, yet became sin for us. Thank you for allowing his head to be bloodied by that thorny crown, so that you could lift up our heads and crown us with your steadfast love and mercy. Thank you for your deep and infinite love that willingly crushed your only Son so that his wounds could pay our ransom. Dear Father, thank you that our sin is dealt with, fully paid for, and that we have become the righteous through faith in the work of your Son.

Father, we are desperately weak people who constantly need your help. Please turn our eyes toward your radiant Son to see his head now crowned with glory and honor, always pleading in our defense. Help us remember all the benefits that flow toward us because of our redemption in Christ. Give us such great love for your Son and gratitude to you, that we are transformed into people who want to obey you with all our hearts. Make us children who love with the same kind of love that we have received from you. Cause us to point one another to Christ as our only hope for surviving this fallen world and our own sinful hearts. Thank you that nothing can keep us from reaching our heavenly home, where we will see your Lamb seated on his throne, crowned with radiant glory, where we will fall at his feet and worship for all eternity. Amen.

ASSURANCE OF PARDON: HEBREWS 2:9–10; PSALM 103:1–4

We see him who for a little while was made lower than the angels, namely Jesus, crowned with glory and honor because of the suffering of death, so that by the grace of God he might taste death for everyone.

For it was fitting that he, for whom and by whom all things exist, in bringing many sons to glory, should make the founder of their salvation perfect through suffering.

Bless the LORD, O my soul,
  and all that is within me,
  bless his holy name!
Bless the LORD, O my soul,
  and forget not all his benefits,

who forgives all your iniquity,
  who heals all your diseases,
who redeems your life from the pit,
  who crowns you with steadfast love and mercy.

✥ HYMNS

"Depth of Mercy"
"How Deep the Father's Love"

LOVE FOR ENEMIES (2)

✥ CALL TO CONFESSION: LUKE 6:27–28, 35–36

"But I say to you who hear, Love your enemies, do good to those who hate you, bless those who curse you, pray for those who abuse you. . . .

. . . But love your enemies, and do good, and lend, expecting nothing in return, and your reward will be great, and you will be sons of the Most High, for he is kind to the ungrateful and the evil. Be merciful, even as your Father is merciful."

✥ PRAYER OF CONFESSION

O Lord, our Rock and Fortress,

We are unloving people. We find it difficult to serve our closest friends and family, and impossible to love our enemies without your help. We are quick to hate those who sin against us, finding it easy to seek revenge and harbor bitterness in our hearts. We have lofty expectations of how we want to be treated by others, yet we are easily disappointed or resentful when we are not treated as we think we ought to be. We are slow to be generous to those around us, and when we are, we expect to be richly rewarded for our kindness by you and by them. We come to you as poor sinners full of fear, for your law exposes our hearts and crushes our pride. We cannot love those who abuse us without your intervening Spirit. We cannot be merciful to evil and ungrateful men unless you ravish our hearts with your astounding, sacrificial love.

Lord, thank you for your perfect Son, who loved his enemies even as he was punished for their sin and tortured in their place. He showed tender love to the most evil and ungrateful people, those who were just like us in every way. When Jesus sought refuge in you as he was dying, you looked away and allowed him to be utterly crushed by the mountain of your just demands, so that we can now hide safely in his love and strong salvation. Thank you for the deep and effective love you have for your precious children, and for enabling us to worship and adore your glorious Son, our Servant King.

Father, help us to become kind and merciful lovers of our friends and enemies. Open our eyes to your amazing love and generosity toward us until we are transformed into your image, to love as you love. When we are sinned against, cause us to cherish your great mercy to us and then extend it freely to other wretched sinners like ourselves. May we always see ourselves accurately as helpless sinners in need of grace, so that we never move beyond the cross or consider ourselves better than our worst enemies. Thank you for loving us when we hated you, and for abandoning your precious Son to welcome us into your family forever. Amen.

ASSURANCE OF PARDON: ROMANS 5:6–10

For while we were still weak, at the right time Christ died for the ungodly. For one will scarcely die for a righteous person—though perhaps for a good person one would dare even to die—but God shows his love for us in that while we were still sinners, Christ died for us. Since, therefore, we have now been justified by his blood, much more shall we be saved by him from the wrath of God. For if while we were enemies we were reconciled to God by the death of his Son, much more, now that we are reconciled, shall we be saved by his life.

HYMNS

"Hide Away in the Love of Jesus"
"Poor Sinner Dejected with Fear"
"The Servant King"

GREAT FORGIVENESS

✥ CALL TO CONFESSION: LUKE 7:36–38, 44–47

One of the Pharisees asked [Jesus] to eat with him, and he went into the Pharisee's house and reclined at the table. And behold, a woman of the city, who was a sinner, when she learned that he was reclining at table in the Pharisee's house, brought an alabaster flask of ointment, and standing behind him at his feet, weeping, she began to wet his feet with her tears and wiped them with the hair of her head and kissed his feet and anointed them with the ointment. . . .

. . . Then turning toward the woman he said to Simon, "Do you see this woman? I entered your house; you gave me no water for my feet, but she has wet my feet with her tears and wiped them with her hair. You gave me no kiss, but from the time I came in she has not ceased to kiss my feet. You did not anoint my head with oil, but she has anointed my feet with ointment. Therefore I tell you, her sins, which are many, are forgiven—for she loved much. But he who is forgiven little, loves little."

✥ PRAYER OF CONFESSION

King of creation,

We come to you as our deliverer, confessing our inability to love and forgive. Like Simon the Pharisee, we are confused by our own so-called goodness. We often judge others for their sins, particularly the sins that affect us. We hold the sins of others against them, even when they have repented of them, speaking badly of them and considering ourselves better than them. When we have been genuinely sinned against and the person is not repentant, we cut them off from our lives. We do not pray for them, we do not wish that they be restored to you and delivered from their sin, and we certainly do not love them. Like Simon, we love little.

Yet we have been forgiven so much. Our unwillingness to forgive, our hardness of heart, and our selfishness are exactly what Jesus had to die for on the cross. Draw us near to this scene,

Lord. As you looked upon your Son when he became sin for us, you saw our unforgiving spirit, our inability to love, our selfish desire to establish kingdoms where our will is done. Yet Jesus was the one upon whom your just and holy wrath was poured out. It was our sin that nailed him there, our sin that you punished, our sin that left Jesus forsaken by you. Yet we are given the credit of one who did nothing that ever needed to be forgiven. When you look upon us, we are given the status of sons and daughters who love consistently, selflessly, and perfectly, because this is exactly how Jesus lived on our behalf.

In light of this gospel, Father, we see that we are without excuse. We have been forgiven a vast debt. We should be left in wonder and gratitude for the immeasurable love you have shown us. Help us by your Spirit to know these truths deeply in our hearts. Change us, we pray, into those who love much, because we have been loved so deeply. Make us sons and daughters who forgive with sincerity and with the desire to restore, so that we might reflect our glorious Savior, who forgave us at such a great cost to himself. Lead us home, Lord, where we will no longer struggle against this unforgiving, unloving flesh, but fellowship together in the perfect unity that you have prepared for us in Christ. Amen.

ASSURANCE OF PARDON: LUKE 7:48–50

And he said to her, "Your sins are forgiven." Then those who were at table with him began to say among themselves, "Who is this, who even forgives sins?" And he said to the woman, "Your faith has saved you; go in peace."

HYMNS

"Jesus, Keep Me Near the Cross"
"Rock of Ages"

THE CROSS

✥ CALL TO CONFESSION: LUKE 9:23–24

And [Jesus] said to all, "If anyone would come after me, let him deny himself and take up his cross daily and follow me. For whoever would save his life will lose it, but whoever loses his life for my sake will save it."

✥ PRAYER OF CONFESSION

Wonderful Savior,

We thank you for your wondrous grace and love in bearing our sin in your own body on the cross. May your cross be to us the tree that sweetens every bitterness in our lives; the rod that blossoms with hope and beauty; the vine that connects us to you, the only source of all our strength. We have died with you, have risen with you, and are even now seated with you in heavenly places. Yet we find that sin continues to have great power over us in our daily lives. Selfishness is in the very fabric of our flesh, and we struggle to choose love for others over pleasing ourselves. When we do manage to serve others, we often take pride in our own good conduct. Father, forgive us for the self-gratifying and self-exalting lives we lead.

Jesus, thank you for giving up the glory of heaven to please your Father, and to rescue us. You denied yourself the adoration you deserved to enter a world full of people who would reject you. You willingly carried the enormous burden of our sinfulness and carried it throughout your life. You lived a life of self-denial and sacrificial love for others, always obeying your Father. We thank you for your radiant robe of righteousness that replaces the filthy and shredded rags of our attempts to be good. You took our sin to the cross and paid the full price we owed, so that we could be free from bondage to sin and death, and from our relentless self-worship, and we are so thankful for this immeasurable gift.

Holy Spirit, we have been given a cross to carry before we wear the crown. We confess that self-love causes us to reproach that cross, and human reason leads us to run from it. Remind us that Jesus has carried that cross already for us, and he will surely carry it with us from day to day. Increase our joy in the cross of Christ, and our wonder and admiration for all that was accomplished there, until our hearts melt and our self-worship gives way to delight in our salvation. As true worship fills our souls, may we grow into people who swiftly turn away from our own desires to love others as we have been so greatly loved. We pray in the name of our glorious Redeemer, amen.

✥ ASSURANCE OF PARDON: JOHN 10:17–18, 27–29; 15:13

"For this reason the Father loves me, because I lay down my life that I may take it up again. No one takes it from me, but I lay it down of my own accord. I have authority to lay it down, and I have authority to take it up again. This charge I have received from my Father."

. . . "My sheep hear my voice, and I know them, and they follow me. I give them eternal life, and they will never perish, and no one will snatch them out of my hand. My Father, who has given them to me, is greater than all, and no one is able to snatch them out of the Father's hand."

✥✥✥

"Greater love has no one than this, that someone lay down his life for his friends."

✥ HYMNS

"Hide Away in the Love of Jesus"
"Jesus Be My All"

PRIDE

✣ CALL TO CONFESSION: LUKE 11:37–41

While Jesus was speaking, a Pharisee asked him to dine with him, so he went in and reclined at table. The Pharisee was astonished to see that he did not first wash before dinner. And the Lord said to him, "Now you Pharisees cleanse the outside of the cup and of the dish, but inside you are full of greed and wickedness. You fools! Did not he who made the outside make the inside also? But give as alms those things that are within, and behold, everything is clean for you."

✣ PRAYER OF CONFESSION

Precious heavenly Father,

It is difficult to see the Pharisee within ourselves, and painful to admit how hypocritical and judgmental we really are. We see the sins of others with crystal clarity, yet are deceived and mesmerized daily by our own outward goodness. We excel at performing for the applause of a watching world, while ignoring and hiding the foul cesspool of wickedly sinful thoughts that dominate our minds for most of the day, every day. We lust, covet, and exalt ourselves constantly. We steal your glory by taking credit for your work in our lives, and create entire kingdoms in our imaginations where we are worshiped instead of you. In this we have offended your holiness and committed treason against you in every corner of our depraved hearts and minds.

Kind and holy Jesus, your glowing righteousness rescues us from our wickedness and greed. You never performed for others or lived to impress them. You were perfect in honesty and truth from the inside out, and even now your radiant goodness replaces all our sin and disobedience. In your perfection, you had every right to judge and humiliate sinners around you, yet you dearly loved the most sinful of humans and forgave them freely. Our guilt and treason were your undoing, yet even now you think of us with loving pity and unswerving devotion. Jesus, thank you for living and dying for each one of us.

Powerful Holy Spirit, put to death the Pharisee in our souls. Give us true and sober judgment about ourselves, and honest courage to admit what incredible sinners we really are. Convict us daily of our sin and of our goodness, of which we are so proud, and never let us escape from our need of a Savior. Help us to live a life of honesty before others, confessing our sin and asking for their help to see more clearly. Rescue us from the love of our own reputation, and change our hearts, we pray. Cause us to see Jesus daily, to love him deeply, and to become like him as we adore him in all his brilliant glory. Amen.

✥ ASSURANCE OF PARDON: HEBREWS 9:13–14

For if the blood of goats and bulls, and the sprinkling of defiled persons with the ashes of a heifer, sanctify for the purification of the flesh, how much more will the blood of Christ, who through the eternal Spirit offered himself without blemish to God, purify our conscience from dead works to serve the living God.

✥ HYMNS

"Ah, Holy Jesus"
"Blessed Assurance"

LIGHT OF THE WORLD

✥ CALL TO CONFESSION: JOHN 1:1–5

In the beginning was the Word, and the Word was with God, and the Word was God. He was in the beginning with God. All things were made through him, and without him was not any thing made that was made. In him was life, and the life was the light of men. The light shines in the darkness, and the darkness has not overcome it.

✥ PRAYER OF CONFESSION

Mighty God,

You are the great Creator, who has made all things from nothing. In the beginning you made man in your image and declared all your handiwork to be good. You took pleasure in your creation, crowning it with the light of your presence as you walked with Adam in the garden each day. But Adam fell, exchanging the glorious light of your love for the darkness of sin and rebellion; each one of us sinned in Adam, and we continue to sin. We are lovers of darkness as we hide ourselves from you in guilt and despair. We thank you that our sin and darkness can never overwhelm the shining brightness of your glory. Though we still are drawn to walk in darkness many times each day, you sent your Son into this world to shine the radiant light of your love on vile sinners like us. Thank you, Lord.

Jesus, all things were made through you. You are worthy of the worship of angels, yet you laid aside your crown and took on our flesh in order to destroy our darkness. Born as a helpless babe, you are the Messiah who came to redeem us from the fall and reconcile us to God. Though you were the Light of the World, you were slain by darkness in order to satisfy the wrath of your Father as you paid for the sin of your people. Then bursting forth from the darkness of death, you rose again into the glorious light of day and victoriously carried our human flesh and blood into the courts of heaven. There in heaven, those you have redeemed will worship you forever as Savior and King.

Holy Spirit, draw our hearts from darkness to light. Show us the glory of our Redeemer and cause us to revel in his love and bask in the warmth and joy of his great pleasure in us. Cause us to hate the darkness of our sin and flee to the brightness of his love, which welcomes us as treasured family members and carries us as honored guests to the table of celebration. We come in his holy name, amen.

✥ ASSURANCE OF PARDON: JOHN 1:14, 16–18

And the Word became flesh and dwelt among us, and we have seen his glory, glory as of the only Son from the Father, full of grace and truth. . . . For from his fullness we have all received, grace upon grace. For the law was given through Moses; grace and truth came through Jesus Christ. No one has ever seen God; the only God, who is at the Father's side, he has made him known.

✥ HYMNS

"Carried to the Table"
"In Christ Alone"
"The Son of God Came Down"

LOVE (1)

✥ CALL TO CONFESSION: JOHN 13:34–35

"A new commandment I give to you, that you love one another: just as I have loved you, you also are to love one another. By this all people will know that you are my disciples, if you have love for one another."

✥ PRAYER OF CONFESSION

God of glory and love,

You have loved us from the beginning with a vast and boundless love. Before we took our first breath, your Son breathed his last and accomplished what we never could: our full and free salvation. You endured the searing loss of your most precious treasure to pay our ransom, and for this we adore you today with joy and gladness. You have called us to love one another as you have loved us, and we confess before you our complete unwillingness to obey this command. Like Cain, we are often consumed with jealousy of our brothers and sisters, harboring deep hatred in our hearts toward them. Instead of laying down our lives for others, we require them to serve us, and resent them when they fail to meet our expectations. Forgive us, Lord.

Jesus, we thank you that we can have confidence before your Father because your blood has purified us from our sin. You endured the deep and boundless anger of your Father so that his love and approval would flow over us endlessly. You took on our humanity and loved others on our behalf, forgiving and confronting people around you with sacrificial and generous compassion. You freely gave your life to provide us with a new record, and in you we have become lovers of others and commandment keepers. Thank you, Jesus, for your shining goodness that dresses us in glory to stand before the King.

Holy Spirit, we need your strength and help to survive our many failures to love others every day. Please give us swift and true repentance for our very real hatred toward others. Convict us of our selfishness and pride, and soften our hearts to cherish and love one another. Help us to believe that you love us, and cause that love to transform us radically into people who extend grace and mercy to others. Let us see the cross more clearly and more often, where the power of your love is openly displayed, where our sin is crushed and destroyed, and where our names are written in the wounds of our crucified Savior. We come in his name, amen.

✥ ASSURANCE OF PARDON: 1 JOHN 4:9–10

In this the love of God was made manifest among us, that God sent his only Son into the world, so that we might live through him. In this is love, not that we have loved God but that he loved us and sent his Son to be the propitiation for our sins.

✥ HYMNS

"How Deep the Father's Love"
"Poor Sinner Dejected with Fear"
"The Power of the Cross"

TROUBLED HEARTS

✥ CALL TO CONFESSION: JOHN 14:1–3

"Let not your hearts be troubled. Believe in God; believe also in me. In my Father's house are many rooms. If it were not so, would I have told you that I go to prepare a place for you? And if I go and prepare a place for you, I will come again and will take you to myself, that where I am you may be also."

✥ PRAYER OF CONFESSION

Heavenly Father,

Many of us come before you today with troubled hearts and minds. We are fearful about our relationships, our health, our finances, our families, our futures, and many other things. We have a hard time believing in you in a way that would bring comfort to our hearts. Instead we greatly doubt your love and concern for us, and sometimes even your very existence. We are not calmed by the thought that you have prepared a place for us in heaven. Father, forgive our unbelief.

Jesus, thank you for your fearless faith. Thank you that for the joy that was set before you, you persevered through far greater pain and suffering than anything we will ever suffer—in fact, through greater pain and suffering than we can even imagine. Thank you that you will come back and take us to be with you forever, wiping away all our tears and comforting at last our grieving and broken hearts.

Holy Spirit, help us to believe in Christ. Help us to believe that in his death we died, and that in his resurrection we are raised to new life. Give us the joy and peace that should flow from that reality, as we continue to face the broken world in which we live, especially as we face the last enemy, death itself. Help us to live in the light of our full forgiveness, and to die with great confidence in the sufficiency of your grace to us in Jesus Christ. In his name, we pray, amen.

✥ ASSURANCE OF PARDON: JOHN 11:25–26; 3:16

Jesus said to her, "I am the resurrection and the life. Whoever believes in me, though he die, yet shall he live, and everyone who lives and believes in me shall never die. Do you believe this?"

✥✥✥

"For God so loved the world, that he gave his only Son, that whoever believes in him should not perish but have eternal life."

✥ HYMNS

"Abide with Me"
"Christ the Lord Is Risen Today"

DOUBT

✣ CALL TO CONFESSION: JOHN 20:24–25

Now Thomas, one of the Twelve, called the Twin, was not with them when Jesus came. So the other disciples told him, "We have seen the Lord." But he said to them, "Unless I see in his hands the mark of the nails, and place my finger into the mark of the nails, and place my hand into his side, I will never believe."

✣ PRAYER OF CONFESSION

Merciful Father,

We come to confess our incredible lack of faith in the reality of the resurrection. Like Thomas, we often live in defiant doubt of your resurrection, evidenced by our idolatrous and self-centered lives. It is shocking and almost inconceivable that you would allow your Son to bear the just and holy wrath that was reserved for us, even to the point of death. Yet you have sealed the promise of our forgiveness and perfect salvation by raising him from the grave, victorious over death and hell itself. This amazing truth is what we have doubted. Forgive us, Lord, for this abuse of your priceless gift. We confess that when we sin with our bodies, minds, and spirits, we live as though Christ never left the tomb. We live in the deadness of our flesh as though you too are dead. Deliver us from this living death, we pray.

Suffering, victorious Savior, you never doubted your Father. Even as you experienced the agony of being abandoned by him on the cross, you trusted your Father to keep his promise to you and raise you from the dead. Now your perfect faith is ours, and we live confidently in the joy of your obedience credited to us. Although we walk through this life as poor, wretched, and needy sinners, we are clothed with your goodness, and we are participants in your endless victory over death.

Powerful Holy Spirit, help us to be children who live by faith, and not by sight. Impress upon us the reality of what we cannot see—Jesus' hands in heaven, forever bearing scars that proclaim that the punishment of our sins has been paid in full. Transform us into people who do not doubt you. Help us to believe firmly in the power of the cross. Strengthen us to become people of growing faith who hate our sin and run from it until love's redeeming work is completely finished. Raise our joys and triumphs high as we wait for that day when we will follow where Christ has led, be made like him, and worship our risen Savior forever. Amen.

✥ ASSURANCE OF PARDON: JOHN 20:26–28

Eight days later, his disciples were inside again, and Thomas was with them. Although the doors were locked, Jesus came and stood among them and said, "Peace be with you." Then he said to Thomas, "Put your finger here, and see my hands; and put out your hand, and place it in my side. Do not disbelieve, but believe." Thomas answered him, "My Lord and my God!"

✥ HYMNS

"All I Have Is Christ"
"Behold the Lamb"
"Christ the Lord is Risen Today"
"The Power of the Cross"
"What the Lord Has Done in Me"

FALSE WORSHIP

✦ CALL TO CONFESSION: ROMANS 1:20–23

For [God's] invisible attributes, namely, his eternal power and divine nature, have been clearly perceived, ever since the creation of the world, in the things that have been made. So they are without excuse. For although they knew God, they did not honor him as God or give thanks to him, but they became futile in their thinking, and their foolish hearts were darkened. Claiming to be wise, they became fools, and exchanged the glory of the immortal God for images resembling mortal man and birds and animals and creeping things.

✦ PRAYER OF CONFESSION

Immortal God,

You are the all-wise King who created and sustains all things by your wisdom. You have revealed your glory and majestic power in the world all around us. Your fingerprints in creation are unmistakable for all those who are willing to look. Your holiness and power are made evident in your providential care for everything you have made, including us. Yet we confess that we have not honored you and given you the thanks and praise you deserve. Instead of worshiping you, we have worshiped power, control, sex, money, reputation, and many other things. We have praised and valued these things above all in our hearts, pursuing them as if they were treasure. We have respected and honored people who were successful in serving these idols while ignoring and mocking others who were faithful to you. These things are not worthy of our worship: they cannot save us and protect us from our enemies, nor can they transform us into pure and holy people.

Lord Jesus, thank you for your pure and wise worship of your heavenly Father. You never flinched from glorifying your Father, growing daily in knowledge and wisdom and the fear of the Lord. When Satan tempted you in the wilderness, you refused to bow down to him, instead reminding him of God's Word, which says,

"You shall worship the Lord your God, and him only shall you serve" (Luke 4:8). Thank you that your faithful obedience and holy wisdom are reckoned to us as our righteousness before your Father.

Holy Spirit, make wisdom delightful to the inmost parts of our souls. Draw us daily to the cross, which is the most powerful demonstration of the wisdom of God. Show us the perfect life that Christ has lived for us, and then shape us so that we can turn away increasingly from the seductive power of the wisdom of this world and receive in its place biblical wisdom. Grow us daily in the knowledge and fear of the Lord, until you complete that good work on the day you take us to be with you forever in heaven. In the name of Christ we pray, amen.

✥ ASSURANCE OF PARDON: 1 CORINTHIANS 1:21–25

For since, in the wisdom of God, the world did not know God through wisdom, it pleased God through the folly of what we preach to save those who believe. For Jews demand signs and Greeks seek wisdom, but we preach Christ crucified, a stumbling block to Jews and folly to Gentiles, but to those who are called, both Jews and Greeks, Christ the power of God and the wisdom of God. For the foolishness of God is wiser than men, and the weakness of God is stronger than men.

✥ HYMNS

"All I Have Is Christ"
"Beneath the Cross of Jesus"
"Immortal, Invisible, God Only Wise"

BONDAGE TO SIN (1)

✥ CALL TO CONFESSION: ROMANS 7:6; 13:12–14

But now we are released from the law, having died to that which held us captive, so that we serve in the new way of the Spirit and not in the old way of the written code.

✥✥✥

The night is far gone; the day is at hand. So then let us cast off the works of darkness and put on the armor of light. Let us walk properly as in the daytime, not in orgies and drunkenness, not in sexual immorality and sensuality, not in quarreling and jealousy. But put on the Lord Jesus Christ, and make no provision for the flesh, to gratify its desires.

✥ PRAYER OF CONFESSION

Holy Father,

Our love of sin also astounds us. Whether we have known you for many years or are babies in faith, it is still our nature to sin. Our affections are turned away from you, and none of our desires or motivations is pure. Though we have died to the eternal consequences of sin, we often choose to live as slaves to lust and selfishness, doing things we know we should not, and failing to do things we should. We medicate ourselves against pain in many sinful ways, and our minds are full of dark and dangerous imaginings. We despise our weakness and inability to change ourselves, so we continue to try to reform, to prove to you that we are worth loving, worth having, worth keeping. Father, have mercy on us; Father, forgive us.

Jesus, though our sins are vast in number, you are more than adequate for our relief. As our re-Creator, you have provided all that is necessary for our salvation. Though our guilt rises to condemn us, your righteousness soars above it to plead on our behalf. Each sin is paid for—past, present, and future—and your perfect record of holiness is credited to us. We are so thankful for your sacrificial love.

Holy Spirit, renew our minds with the truth of the gospel, and melt our hearts with the reality of how we have been cherished in Christ. Help us not to use grace as an excuse to sin. Delight and ravish us by the love of our Savior until our hearts change and we desire obedience to him above everything else. May the joy of the gospel free us to put off sin and put on obedience. We praise you that your sanctifying work cannot be stopped or delayed, by us, by others, or by Satan himself. Your plan is to make all things new, and although in this world we will only make small beginnings, a day is coming when we will be new creations, inside and out, and stand before you in sinless perfection. Until that day, may the sweet rest we have in the work of Christ give us fresh courage and strength to engage the daily battle with our sinful hearts with gratitude and joy. In the strong name of Jesus we pray, amen.

ASSURANCE OF PARDON: GALATIANS 3:26–29

In Christ Jesus you are all sons of God, through faith. For as many of you as were baptized into Christ have put on Christ. There is neither Jew nor Greek, there is neither slave nor free, there is no male and female, for you are all one in Christ Jesus. And if you are Christ's, then you are Abraham's offspring, heirs according to promise.

HYMNS

"And Can It Be"
"I'll Rest in Christ"
"Not What My Hands Have Done"

BONDAGE TO SIN (2)

✣ CALL TO CONFESSION: ROMANS 7:19–23

For I do not do the good I want, but the evil I do not want is what I keep on doing. Now if I do what I do not want, it is no longer I who do it, but sin that dwells within me.

So I find it to be a law that when I want to do right, evil lies close at hand. For I delight in the law of God, in my inner being, but I see in my members another law waging war against the law of my mind and making me captive to the law of sin that dwells in my members.

✣ PRAYER OF CONFESSION

O Lord, our helper,

We are people who often run toward sin instead of running away from it. We fix our eyes on our own desires and pursue them recklessly with no thought of danger to our souls. We are overconfident, thinking that we can resist sin, only to discover that we are far weaker than we ever imagined. Sometimes we want to do good and are unable to carry it out, and other times we do not even want to do what we know is good. We love your law in theory, but in practice we wage war against your perfect law and sin against you often in our thoughts and deeds. We know that we are free from the bondage of sin, yet we choose to live as slaves to sin, addicted to our destructive habits and the things that make us feel good. Father, forgive us.

Jesus, thank you for faithfully choosing the freedom of obedience over the slavery of sin. You cherished sinners without ever joining them in their disobedience, and you loved and kept your Father's law perfectly in our place. Your sacrificial death has broken the power of sin in us, and the power of the law over us, and we are deeply grateful. Our sinful souls are counted free because of your righteous life and ransoming death, and now we are truly free to approach you with joy and confidence. Thank you for your amazing grace that draws us irresistibly before your throne to worship you, not as slaves but as children of the living God.

Holy Spirit, free us increasingly from our voluntary slavery to sin. Melt our hearts with the overwhelming kindness and love of God, until we long to obey your law with all our heart, mind, soul, and strength. Help us to believe that you effectively love desperate sinners like us, and that you will never let us go. Cause us to rest in the perfect goodness of Jesus Christ as our only hope, and grant us growing obedience that springs from deep gratitude for all you have done for us. May we hear the words, "no condemnation," and know in our hearts that we have been freed from the bondage of sin, that our chains are gone, and that our hearts are free to worship you forever. Amen.

ASSURANCE OF PARDON: ROMANS 7:24–25; 8:1–2

Wretched man that I am! Who will deliver me from this body of death? Thanks be to God through Jesus Christ our Lord!

There is therefore now no condemnation for those who are in Christ Jesus. For the law of the Spirit of life has set you free in Christ Jesus from the law of sin and death.

HYMNS

"Amazing Grace"
"Before the Throne of God Above"
"I Lay My Sins on Jesus"

PRAYER

✥ CALL TO CONFESSION: ROMANS 8:26–27

Likewise the Spirit helps us in our weakness. For we do not know what to pray for as we ought, but the Spirit himself intercedes for us with groanings too deep for words. And he who searches hearts knows what is the mind of the Spirit, because the Spirit intercedes for the saints according to the will of God.

✥ PRAYER OF CONFESSION

Heavenly Father,

Teach us to love prayer. Help us to live our lives before you, in public and in private, at church and at home, each prayer and each moment perfumed with the incense of Christ's atoning blood. We are invited by your promises to come to you with all our burdens and desires. Draw us by the power of your Spirit, or our hearts and minds will wander carelessly from thought to thought, and our anxieties will rule over us.

We praise you that great sin draws out great grace, for we are great sinners. We seldom want to pray, and when we do our petitions are laced with self-importance and mixed with sinful motives. We confess our ignorance, for we do not know how to pray, and we confess our willful rebellion for prayers uttered from cold and selfish lips. But we celebrate Jesus and plead his righteousness to cover our iniquities, and rejoice that his obedience weighs more heavily on your scales than all our sin and satisfies your justice in full. Where our guilt is most terrible, your mercy is most free and deep, and we thank you for this incredible grace.

Holy Spirit, by your power, may the throne of grace become the pleasure ground of our souls. There may we know the delight of our Savior's love, the relief of repentance and reconciliation, the privilege of our sonship. Ignite our hearts with joy before you, quicken our deadness with thanksgiving, and strengthen us to cling to you, love you, and obey you. Fill us with the imagination of faith, which considers all things possible and believes that you are a God who loves to give far beyond all that we could ask or imagine. May we grow to be persistent in prayer, until Christ is the pulse of our hearts, the spokesman of our lips, and the center of all our hopes and longings. In his great name we pray, amen.

✣ ASSURANCE OF PARDON: ROMANS 16:25–27

Now to him who is able to strengthen you according to my gospel and the preaching of Jesus Christ, according to the revelation of the mystery that was kept secret for long ages but has now been disclosed and through the prophetic writings has been made known to all nations, according to the command of the eternal God, to bring about the obedience of faith—to the only wise God be glory forevermore through Jesus Christ! Amen.

✣ HYMNS

"Spirit of God, Descend upon My Heart"
"Wonderful, Merciful Savior"

GOD'S PROVISION

✣ CALL TO CONFESSION: ROMANS 8:28

And we know that for those who love God all things work together for good, for those who are called according to his purpose.

✣ PRAYER OF CONFESSION

Mighty God, our Rock and our Shield,

You are our deliverer and our refuge from danger. We know we have nothing to fear in life or in death, yet we do fear. You have told us to rest from our own striving, yet we often rely on our own strength and find ourselves consumed with anxiety and deeply shaken by this world and by our own weakness. You have promised to work all things in this universe together for our spiritual blessing and good, yet we doubt your love and argue with your wisdom. We read of your faithfulness to Abraham and Sarah as a promise-keeping God, but we wonder if you will still be faithful to us, their children. Father, forgive us for our unbelief and pride, which cause us repeatedly to doubt your love, your Word, and your power to hold onto us and work all things together for our good.

Lord, thank you that in the midst of our faltering belief, you have provided a strong and powerful Savior. Though Satan's accusations ring in our ears and threaten to undo us, you have declared us righteous and blameless in your sight because of Christ. You are the Great King of the universe. Silence our mouths when we condemn ourselves, and settle our frightened souls when we tremble with fear before you. Persuade us day after day that you are always on our side, even when we grieve you by a thousand falls. Show us how your wrath toward our sin has been emptied on your precious Son, and let us feel deeply in our souls that Jesus has paid for every sin with his bleeding wounds.

Holy Spirit, guide us through this barren, desert land with your powerful hand. Give us eyes to see our Savior, pleading for us as he bears deep wounds that proclaim, "No condemnation." Give us growing faith to believe in your relentless love for us, and strong minds to discern your truth from Satan's lies. Please grant us joyful hope to long for heaven, and grace to find rest and contentment in you on our journey there. In Christ's name we pray, amen.

✣ ASSURANCE OF PARDON: ROMANS 8:31–34

What then shall we say to these things? If God is for us, who can be against us? He who did not spare his own Son but gave him up for us all, how will he not also with him graciously give us all things? Who shall bring any charge against God's elect? It is God who justifies. Who is to condemn? Christ Jesus is the one who died—more than that, who was raised—who is at the right hand of God, who indeed is interceding for us.

✣ HYMNS

"Depth of Mercy"
"Guide Me, O Thou Great Jehovah"

GOD'S SOVEREIGNTY

✥ CALL TO CONFESSION: ROMANS 9:14–24

What shall we say then? Is there injustice on God's part? By no means! For he says to Moses, "I will have mercy on whom I have mercy, and I will have compassion on whom I have compassion." So then it depends not on human will or exertion, but on God, who has mercy. For the Scripture says to Pharaoh, "For this very purpose I have raised you up, that I might show my power in you, and that my name might be proclaimed in all the earth." So then he has mercy on whomever he wills, and he hardens whomever he wills.

You will say to me then, "Why does he still find fault? For who can resist his will?" But who are you, O man, to answer back to God? Will what is molded say to its molder, "Why have you made me like this?" Has the potter no right over the clay, to make out of the same lump one vessel for honorable use and another for dishonorable use? What if God, desiring to show his wrath and to make known his power, has endured with much patience vessels of wrath prepared for destruction, in order to make known the riches of his glory for vessels of mercy, which he has prepared beforehand for glory—even us whom he has called, not from the Jews only but also from the Gentiles?

✥ PRAYER OF CONFESSION

Sovereign Lord,

We praise you for loving us while we were still your enemies, and for choosing us to belong to you before the foundation of the world. We adore the wonders of your condescending love that stooped to save us from our sad and sinful state, and rescue us from the hell we deserve. Thank you for calling us to life in you, and for giving us the faith and strength to obey that call and run to you for relief from all our sin and shame. You have given us life and have ravished our hateful and rebellious hearts with your astounding and irresistible love. We are undone by the depth of your mercy and kindness.

Even so, almighty God, we are clay pots who are quick to argue with you, our Creator and Defender. We have no right to talk back to you, yet we often consider your ways unjust and imagine ourselves to be more wise and kind than you are. When the truth of your character and Word humble us and contradict our desires, our anger rises up before you and we charge you with imaginary crimes. Forgive us, Lord, for wanting to instruct you in mercy and grace. Thank you for your endless patience with your foolish children. Thank you for the powerful blood of our wonderful Savior, which pays for the sins of all your chosen people. Thank you for his perfect humility and submission to your will, especially when it led him to suffer the agony of the cross, and the unbearable torment of rejection by you. Thank you for clothing us with the righteousness of your Son and seating us at your table of joy and feasting.

Holy Spirit, continue to humble us and fill us with awe and wonder that we should be chosen sons and daughters of the Great King. Give us a vibrant and growing knowledge of your Word, and sweet submission to the wisdom and will of our heavenly Father. Give us swift repentance when our pride causes us to sin, and lead us many times each day to cherish the cross and the sufferings of our Savior. May the enormous penalty required for our sin remind us of the depths of our depravity and silence our boasting lips. Make us trophies of grace who boast endlessly of your amazing and victorious grace to us in Jesus Christ. Amen.

✣ ASSURANCE OF PARDON: 1 PETER 2:9–10

But you are a chosen race, a royal priesthood, a holy nation, a people for his own possession, that you may proclaim the excellencies of him who called you out of darkness into his marvelous light. Once you were not a people, but now you are God's people; once you had not received mercy, but now you have received mercy.

✣ HYMNS

"Carried to the Table"
"How Sweet and Awesome Is the Place"
"Jesus Be My All"
"Wonderful, Merciful Savior"

SLOTH

✤ CALL TO CONFESSION: ROMANS 12:11; 13:11–12

Do not be slothful in zeal, be fervent in spirit, serve the Lord.

✤✤✤

Besides this you know the time, that the hour has come for you to wake from sleep. For salvation is nearer to us now than when we first believed. The night is far gone; the day is at hand. So then let us cast off the works of darkness and put on the armor of light.

✤ PRAYER OF CONFESSION

Almighty and powerful God,

Forgive us for the way that we have neglected and misused the good gifts that you have given us. We have slept carelessly, when we should have been wide awake. We have shunned opportunities to serve you and find sweet fellowship in your presence when we should have faithfully followed your call. We have loved comfort and ease, and things of little lasting significance, instead of investing our lives in the pursuit of you and your eternal kingdom. We also repent today for all the ways in which we have served you with sinful attitudes, glorying in our own strength and becoming proud of our hard work for you, or resenting bitterly the need to put ourselves out for others. Whether we have worked hard or been lazy, our eyes have been fixed only on ourselves. Father, forgive us.

Jesus, thank you for your good works during your life here on earth, works that were constantly rooted and grounded in faith. You worked hard for your Father's kingdom, but you also rested, knowing that your Father's will would always be done. You were patient with your confused and selfish disciples, and you continue to show enduring mercy to us. You ultimately laid down your life on the cross, so that we might enter the eternal rest that your Father has prepared for all those who trust in you.

Thank you that those good works in our place enable us to stand forgiven in your presence today.

Holy Spirit, stir up our hearts to love and good works. Give us a fervent spirit that delights to pour out our lives in service to you and those around us. Help us to fix our eyes on the glory of your dawning kingdom, and increasingly to put off the old works of darkness. Clothe us in your armor of light, so that even weak and faint followers like us may stand firm in your power, strengthened by you to run and not be weary, to walk and not faint. Help us to see that your grace alone speaks pardon to our weary souls. In Jesus' name we pray, amen.

ASSURANCE OF PARDON: HEBREWS 12:1–3

Therefore, since we are surrounded by so great a cloud of witnesses, let us also lay aside every weight, and sin which clings so closely, and let us run with endurance the race that is set before us, looking to Jesus, the founder and perfecter of our faith, who for the joy that was set before him endured the cross, despising the shame, and is seated at the right hand of the throne of God.

Consider him who endured from sinners such hostility against himself, so that you may not grow weary or fainthearted.

HYMNS

"I'll Rest in Christ"
"Not What My Hands Have Done"

UNITY

✥ CALL TO CONFESSION: 1 CORINTHIANS 12:12–20; PSALM 133:1

For just as the body is one and has many members, and all the members of the body, though many, are one body, so it is with Christ. For in one Spirit we were all baptized into one body—Jews or Greeks, slaves or free—and all were made to drink of one Spirit.

For the body does not consist of one member but of many. If the foot should say, "Because I am not a hand, I do not belong to the body," that would not make it any less a part of the body. And if the ear should say, "Because I am not an eye, I do not belong to the body," that would not make it any less a part of the body. If the whole body were an eye, where would be the sense of hearing? If the whole body were an ear, where would be the sense of smell? But as it is, God arranged the members in the body, each one of them, as he chose. If all were a single member, where would the body be? As it is, there are many parts, yet one body.

✥✥✥

Behold, how good and pleasant it is
when brothers dwell in unity!

✥ PRAYER OF CONFESSION

Triune God,

You are one God in three persons, a diverse unity in whom there is neither division nor contention. You call us also to be one body made up of many different members, with different gifts and abilities, as well as different needs and failings. We confess that we often take pride in our own gifts and look down on those who lack them, while thinking little about our need for the gifts of others in the body. We form factions and cliques that promote and support our own interests, desperately trying to attract the favor of those whom we think strong, while despising and shunning those whom we see as weak, unattractive, or broken. Father, forgive us.

Jesus, thank you for your willingness to allow your physical body to be shattered and broken to establish the unity of your spiritual body, the church. Thank you that in you we have a unity that transcends all earthly boundaries: in you, there is neither Jew nor Gentile, male nor female, slave nor free. Thank you for the particular love and care that you bestowed on the weakest and most ignored members of your community, especially women, children, and outcasts. By your gracious attention, you gave honor to those who lacked it. As the only mediator between us and the Father, you unite all your people in yourself.

Holy Spirit, you are the one who gives each of us our various gifts and callings. Help us to see and appreciate your work in other Christians, honoring them more highly than ourselves. Remove our stony, self-centered hearts and give us hearts of flesh that love our brothers and sisters in Christ and value them just as they are. Teach us to love them with all their weaknesses and sins, as beloved children of our own heavenly Father and servants of the same Master. Bind us firmly together into one new people, united by Christ's work on the cross and your continuing work in each of our hearts. Amen.

✤ ASSURANCE OF PARDON: JOHN 17:20–24

"I do not ask for these only, but also for those who will believe in me through their word, that they may all be one, just as you, Father, are in me, and I in you, that they also may be in us, so that the world may believe that you have sent me. The glory that you have given me I have given to them, that they may be one even as we are one, I in them and you in me, that they may become perfectly one, so that the world may know that you sent me and loved them even as you loved me. Father, I desire that they also, whom you have given me, may be with me where I am, to see my glory that you have given me because you loved me before the foundation of the world."

✤ HYMNS

"I Greet Thee, Who My Sure Redeemer Art"
"There Is a Redeemer"

LOVE (2)

✥ CALL TO CONFESSION: 1 CORINTHIANS 13:1–3

If I speak in the tongues of men and of angels, but have not love, I am a noisy gong or a clanging cymbal. And if I have prophetic powers, and understand all mysteries and all knowledge, and if I have all faith, so as to remove mountains, but have not love, I am nothing. If I give away all I have, and if I deliver up my body to be burned, but have not love, I gain nothing.

✥ PRAYER OF CONFESSION

Holy God,

Forgive us for the countless ways in which we have not loved others. Some of us are very obviously unloving: we are inconsiderate of others' time and rude to those who are not as smart or "holy" as we are; we ignore those whom we do not like, make fun of those that we find tedious or stupid, and choose to maintain perpetually casual relationships so that we do not have to ask questions that make us uncomfortably aware of other people. Others of us are quite good at faking love: we wear ourselves thin with acts of kindness and words of counsel when primarily we are the ones desiring to be loved, we pretend to listen while really we are inwardly condemning others for not being as insightful or as mature as we are, and we make sacrifices for others with conditions that will bring about relational retribution if they are not met. Grief and guilt would leave us in despair over these sins.

Merciful Jesus, you became sinless, perfect man to bear this, our great lack of love. What a wondrous love is this that you would live and die in our place. When you were on earth, you loved others with a specific and meaningful love. You really saw people, not just for what they could give you, but you saw their hearts, their needs, their sorrows, and their sin. You loved us with the greatest love of all: the love that led you to lay down your life to save us. Your loving tongue was silenced, your loving hands were pierced, your loving eyes were closed in death, and your loving heart stopped beating as you were forsaken by your Father to cancel our debt of sin.

Faithful Spirit, we long for Christ's kingdom to come, when we will be fully and finally free from our struggle with self-love and blindness to others. Help us, we pray, to live as citizens of that kingdom now, promoting peace and loving others with the self-sacrificing love that Jesus so perfectly modeled and poured out on us. Help us to want to see others, and help us to listen with our hearts. Continue to change us into those who love without condition, giving grace to others in light of the unimaginable grace that we have been so freely given, which is our only source of change, hope, and life. Amen.

✣ ASSURANCE OF PARDON: 2 CORINTHIANS 5:14–15

For the love of Christ controls us, because we have concluded this: that one has died for all, therefore all have died; and he died for all, that those who live might no longer live for themselves but for him who for their sake died and was raised.

✣ HYMNS

"God, Be Merciful to Me"
"Thy Mercy, My God"
"What Wondrous Love Is This?"

FORGETTING THE GOSPEL

✣ CALL TO CONFESSION: 1 CORINTHIANS 15:1–2

Now I would remind you, brothers, of the gospel I preached to you, which you received, in which you stand, and by which you are being saved, if you hold fast to the word I preached to you—unless you believed in vain.

✣ PRAYER OF CONFESSION

God of all grace,

We are weak and forgetful people, easily distracted by the joys and sorrows of our lives. We are capable of great thoughts concerning you one moment, yet we forget your kindness and live as though we had no hope the next. Forgive us, Father, for the unbelief that clings to our sinful flesh and clouds our minds with doubt and fear.

Jesus, thank you for clinging to us, even though we let go of you repeatedly. You held fast to the gospel in your living, dying, and rising again, always obeying your Father and setting your face toward the hill of sacrifice. You never forgot your mission or resisted your calling, but faithfully lived and died in our place. You endured mocking, beatings, and crucifixion for the joy set before you. Thank you that we are that joy; now fill us with your joy and cause us to find great delight in you. Though we may be quick to forget you and need reminding often, you never forget us. Instead you intercede for us daily before your Father, and you are preparing for the day when we will feast with you in heaven. Come quickly, Lord Jesus!

Holy Spirit, produce in us growing faith that we may live in Christ. May all our desires rest in him constantly. Make Jesus our greatest hope and all our glory. May we enter him as our refuge, build on him as our foundation, walk in him, follow him, conform to him, rely on him, and obey him. Let us never be ashamed of him or his words. May his death comfort us, for we have been loved with unfathomable love. May his resurrection assure us that his obedience was perfect, his sacrifice accepted, and his work finished. Help us to hold fast to the gospel we have believed: to cherish it in our weakness and to profess its power when we stand strong. Deepen our faith and guard our hearts and minds with the helmet of Christ's salvation, the breastplate of his righteousness, the shield of his faith, the sandals of his peace, and the sword of his truth. In his strong name we pray, amen.

✤ ASSURANCE OF PARDON: 1 CORINTHIANS 15:3–4, 21–22

For I delivered to you as of first importance what I also received: that Christ died for our sins in accordance with the Scriptures, that he was buried, that he was raised on the third day in accordance with the Scriptures. . . .

. . . For as by a man came death, by a man has come also the resurrection of the dead. For as in Adam all die, so also in Christ shall all be made alive.

✤ HYMNS

"I'll Rest in Christ"
"Only in the Cross"

RECONCILIATION (1)

✥ CALL TO CONFESSION: 2 CORINTHIANS 5:14–15

For the love of Christ controls us . . . that those who live might no longer live for themselves but for him who for their sake died and was raised.

✥ PRAYER OF CONFESSION

Heavenly Father,

If we deeply understood the cross, gratitude and love for Christ would daily control our thoughts and actions. We are new creations, but we are still great sinners, and this confuses and discourages us. Instead of marveling at your love for weak and sinful creatures, we try to hide our sin and reform ourselves. Rather than seeing each other as gloriously redeemed people, we focus on the weaknesses of others and magnify our own strengths. We spend our days alienated from you and isolated from others, because we reject your sacrifice for our sin and try to substitute our own. We have turned away from you and loved our idols instead, and we have been miserable with ourselves and with others. Instead of living for Christ and calling others to admire and adore him, we have lived small lives that have been governed by our own feelings and desires. Father, forgive us.

Jesus, thank you for invading our world and forever quieting the loud thunder of the law that we cannot keep. You lived the life of grace and mercy that we should live, reconciling your people to one another and to God. Love for your Father compelled you to obedience in spite of great harm to yourself, and by your wounds we have been healed. Jesus, we thank you.

Holy Spirit, help us to think about Jesus whenever our thoughts turn carelessly to self-defense, self-pity, self-glory, and self-condemnation. Use your mighty power to free us from self-love so that we can love others well. Reconcile us to our own weakness so that we will look away from ourselves to Christ often and be drawn into worship and praise. Cause the love of

Christ to control us increasingly as we become more and more persuaded that he loves us. Take our eyes away from the good and bad things that our hands have done, and show us the nail-pierced hands of the one who obeyed and suffered to pay our debt. Teach us to rest in Christ, and make us people who graciously lead others to find rest and peace in him and with one another. Holy Spirit, make us new. Amen.

ASSURANCE OF PARDON: 2 CORINTHIANS 5:17–18, 21

If anyone is in Christ, he is a new creation. The old has passed away; behold, the new has come. All this is from God, who through Christ reconciled us to himself. . . . For our sake he made him to be sin who knew no sin, so that in him we might become the righteousness of God.

HYMNS

"I'll Rest in Christ"
"Let Us Love and Sing and Wonder"
"Not What My Hands Have Done"

DEAD IN SIN

✥ CALL TO CONFESSION: EPHESIANS 2:1–3

And you were dead in the trespasses and sins in which you once walked, following the course of this world, following the prince of the power of the air, the spirit that is now at work in the sons of disobedience—among whom we all once lived in the passions of our flesh, carrying out the desires of the body and the mind, and were by nature children of wrath, like the rest of mankind.

✥ PRAYER OF CONFESSION

Heavenly Father,

We admit to you today that we often live as though we were still dead in our trespasses and sins. You have made us alive in Christ and given us your Holy Spirit, yet our slowly maturing souls dwell in sinful bodies, and we continue to gratify the desires of our flesh in countless ways. We eat too much, drink too much, and indulge in sinful sexual fantasy and practice, medicating ourselves to escape reality and entertaining ourselves to distract from pain. We follow the course of the world around us, giving in to pressure from our friends and our circumstances, instead of living with our eyes fixed on our heavenly home. We frantically fill ourselves up with pleasures, using your good gifts to us as a way to avoid our great need for you. Father, forgive us.

Lord, we wish that we were far more holy than we are. You have told us that we are weak and that our hearts are deceitful and desperately wicked. Thank you that all our sanctification is in your hands. You are the author and perfecter of our faith, and though our remaining sin often shocks us, you are never surprised by it. You have promised that you will use it to show us our great need for you. Give us true grief for our sin and sweet repentance, and then draw us to the cross to find cleansing, healing, and great joy in our salvation. There let us see our Lord and King loving us as the fountain of his blood flowed out for the remission of our sin. Let us celebrate with deep delight the unbelievable love of a Creator who would become like us and submit to the horrors of crucifixion to have us for his own.

Let your voice of sovereign grace drown out the voices of shame and accusation that haunt us. In great peace and in great sorrow, may we grow in faith, in obedience, and in worship before you. Help us to love you more and more and to long with confidence and hope for the day of your return. May the radiant goodness of Jesus in our place be all that we need until we see you face to face. In his precious name we pray, amen.

ASSURANCE OF PARDON: EPHESIANS 2:4–7

But God, being rich in mercy, because of the great love with which he loved us, even when we were dead in our trespasses, made us alive together with Christ—by grace you have been saved—and raised us up with him and seated us with him in the heavenly places in Christ Jesus, so that in the coming ages he might show the immeasurable riches of his grace in kindness toward us in Christ Jesus.

HYMNS

"It Is Well with My Soul"
"Jesus Be My All"

RECONCILIATION (2)

✥ CALL TO CONFESSION: EPHESIANS 2:8–13

For by grace you have been saved through faith. And this is not your own doing; it is the gift of God, not a result of works, so that no one may boast. For we are his workmanship, created in Christ Jesus for good works, which God prepared beforehand, that we should walk in them.

Therefore remember that at one time you Gentiles in the flesh, called "the uncircumcision" by what is called the circumcision, which is made in the flesh by hands—remember that you were at that time separated from Christ, alienated from the commonwealth of Israel and strangers to the covenants of promise, having no hope and without God in the world. But now in Christ Jesus you who once were far off have been brought near by the blood of Christ.

✥ PRAYER OF CONFESSION

Father of mercy,

We marvel today that while we were still sinners, Christ died for us. We were rebels and strangers to you, living in outright opposition to your wisdom and grace, yet you loved us, pursued us, and brought us into your family. You not only forgave our many sins but have lavished us with your love and care, and have promised us unimaginable glory with you forever. Thank you for providing all that was needed to reconcile such determined and hardened sinners to yourself.

Such great love from you should surely melt our hearts with deep love and compassion for other sinners. Yet we confess that we find it hard to forgive those who have hurt us, and difficult to love unlovely people. We expect others to forgive our sins against them and to extend undeserved love toward us, even though we are slow to do the same. Forgive us, Lord, for our hypocrisy. Forgive us for the grudges that we nurse and the memories of past wrongs to which we cling. As you are determined to forget our sins and not hold them against us, so too make us holy forgetters who leave vengeance in your hands and move graciously toward those who have wounded us, whether carelessly or willfully. We ask you to do for us what we cannot do for ourselves, and give us hearts that are like yours, aggressively devoted to forgiveness and reconciliation. Whenever we see a sin in another, may we see it in ourselves as well, and remember how dearly we have been loved by the one whom we have wounded.

Father, we pray that you would surround us with skilled comforters and wise counselors, who will walk alongside us and encourage us in the struggle to forgive. By your Spirit, grant us superhuman hearts of forgiveness in your time. Enable us to live at peace with the reality of relationships that cannot presently be reconciled, remembering that in heaven all will be right. Thank you that, on that day, blind eyes will see clearly, hard hearts will be fully melted, and reconciliation between your people will be complete and enduring. In Jesus' name, amen.

✣ ASSURANCE OF PARDON: EPHESIANS 2:14–22

For he himself is our peace, who has made us both one and has broken down in his flesh the dividing wall of hostility by abolishing the law of commandments expressed in ordinances, that he might create in himself one new man in place of the two, so making peace, and might reconcile us both to God in one body through the cross, thereby killing the hostility. And he came and preached peace to you who were far off and peace to those who were near. For through him we both have access in one Spirit to the Father. So then you are no longer strangers and aliens, but you are fellow citizens with the saints and members of the household of God, built on the foundation of the apostles and prophets, Christ Jesus himself being the cornerstone, in whom the whole structure, being joined together, grows into a holy temple in the Lord. In him you also are being built together into a dwelling place for God by the Spirit.

✣ HYMNS

"The Church's One Foundation"
"I Come by the Blood"

GRACE

✥ CALL TO CONFESSION: EPHESIANS 2:13–19

But now in Christ Jesus you who once were far off have been brought near by the blood of Christ. For he himself is our peace, who has made us both one and has broken down in his flesh the dividing wall of hostility by abolishing the law of commandments expressed in ordinances, that he might create in himself one new man in place of the two, so making peace, and might reconcile us both to God in one body through the cross, thereby killing the hostility. And he came and preached peace to you who were far off and peace to those who were near. For through him we both have access in one Spirit to the Father. So then you are no longer strangers and aliens, but you are fellow citizens with the saints and members of the household of God.

✥ PRAYER OF CONFESSION

Our Father, full of grace and wisdom,

Forgive us for our foolish claims to wisdom, for our misplaced pride in our own weak merits, and for our blind stumbling while claiming to have clear insight. Sometimes we diminish your law through our failure to see the ugliness of our sin and its impact on others, while at other times we diminish your abundant grace through self-focused anxiety about the consequences of our sin. When we appeal to and rest in your grace for ourselves, we often deny it to others, whether their sin is different from ours, or very much the same. Thank you for your mysterious and eternal plan to redeem us through your Son, and for demonstrating your goodness while graciously answering our profound needs as individuals and as a community.

Lord Jesus, thank you for submitting yourself to the Father's plan. You endured the limitations of creaturely existence, and the indignity, pain, and suffering of rejection at the cross for us. You were so very different from us, yet you came near to us and were made like us, so that you might unite us to yourself, to one another, and together through you to the Father and the Spirit.

Thank you for the unsearchable riches of grace, righteousness, wisdom, and free access to God the Father that are now ours through you.

Living Spirit, enlighten our eyes to see the true depth of our sin so that we might begin to know the full and marvelous extent of the grace that we have received. Grant us merciful hearts to extend to others the forgiveness that has been shown to us. Remind us of the free access we have to our Father through Jesus. Convince our doubting hearts of the gospel so strongly that we may boldly and confidently approach the throne with all our joys, all our sorrows, all our confessions, and all our thanks. We come in the powerful name of Christ Jesus, amen.

ASSURANCE OF PARDON: EPHESIANS 2:8–10

For by grace you have been saved through faith. And this is not your own doing; it is the gift of God, not a result of works, so that no one may boast. For we are his workmanship, created in Christ Jesus for good works, which God prepared beforehand, that we should walk in them.

HYMNS

"All I Have Is Christ"
"Forgive Our Sins as We Forgive"

LOVE (3)

✤ CALL TO CONFESSION: EPHESIANS 4:1–3

I therefore, a prisoner for the Lord, urge you to walk in a manner worthy of the calling to which you have been called, with all humility and gentleness, with patience, bearing with one another in love, eager to maintain the unity of the Spirit in the bond of peace.

✤ PRAYER OF CONFESSION

Great Father,

We come before you as deeply stained sinners who have not kept your law. Where your kind and generous law of love has called us to humility, we have been prideful to one another. We hide our weakness and brokenness so that we might not be recognized as the sinners we actually are. Where you have made a holy requirement of gentleness and patience, we have been violent and impatient to one another. Worst of all, where you have urged us to bear with one another in love, we have hated each other: some of us by pointing out others' failures without grace and love, and others of us by rejecting and ignoring people because we simply do not care about them. Yet you have not left us here. What humble, gentle, patient love you have shown us in your Son, Jesus Christ.

Jesus, thank you for the countless times you were humble and gentle with the selfish people swirling around you as you lived your life on this earth. Thank you for every time you responded to others with grace and mercy, with kind words, with sincerity. Jesus, bring us near to your cross, so that we can survey the wonder displayed there: that you would fully and finally bear our burden of sin, so that we might experience unity with you and your Father, and that we might truly find peace.

Holy Spirit, thank you for conviction of sin and for the grand and beautiful gospel to which we may run when we see our sin. Help us to see clearly the ways in which we do not love each other or you, not so that we will be discouraged, but so that we might also clearly see the power and depth of Jesus' love for us. Subdue our remaining sin, we pray. Help us to want to see each other. Cause us to be humble and gentle with one another, help us to be patient, and enable us to bear with one another in love. May we seek help and seek to give it. But, most of all, cause us to remember how our Father sees us: radiantly beautiful, dressed in the righteousness of Jesus. In his name we pray, amen.

✥ ASSURANCE OF PARDON: ISAIAH 53:11–12

> Out of the anguish of his soul he shall see and be satisfied;
> by his knowledge shall the righteous one, my servant,
> make many to be accounted righteous,
> and he shall bear their iniquities.
> Therefore I will divide him a portion with the many,
> and he shall divide the spoil with the strong,
> because he poured out his soul to death
> and was numbered with the transgressors;
> yet he bore the sin of many,
> and makes intercession for the transgressors.

✥ HYMNS

"All I Have Is Christ"
"Jesus Be My All"

TRUTH

✣ CALL TO CONFESSION: EPHESIANS 4:22–25 (NIV)

You were taught, with regard to your former way of life, to put off your old self, which is being corrupted by its deceitful desires; to be made new in the attitude of your minds; and to put on the new self, created to be like God in true righteousness and holiness.

Therefore each of you must put off falsehood and speak truthfully to his neighbor, for we are all members of one body.

✣ PRAYER OF CONFESSION

Sovereign Lord of the universe,

We are harassed by doubts, fears, and unbelief, yet we choose to live in spiritual darkness. Our hearts are full of sinful thoughts and worries, and we cannot create faith in ourselves at all. When we feel that you are absent, we sink into distress and are tempted to many kinds of sin. We lie to protect ourselves, because we do not trust you with our safety, welfare, and reputation. We lie boastfully about ourselves, because we do not trust you to give us the glory that we so crave. We lie to impress people because we fear that you do not love us, so we look to the love and praise of others instead. We lie to escape the consequences of our sin, and we lie to prosper financially because we fear that you will not take care of us. Father, forgive us for the many ways in which we lie to one another, and forgive us for the deep idolatries behind those lies.

Wonderful, merciful Savior, you spoke only truth so that you could give us the perfect righteousness that we need to stand before God without fear. You paid the price for all our falsehood and deceit, our biggest lies and smallest exaggerations. Thank you for your lack of fear of what man could do to you, even when they lied about you and did their worst to you. Thank you for your joyful commitment to love and serve those whom you came to save.

Holy Spirit, renew the spirit of our minds with the truths of the gospel, and help us to put off falsehood and put on truthfulness. Convict us of the many ways in which we lie to others and to ourselves. Show us the fears and idolatries that lead us into sin so that we can repent and worship you in truth. Let us find healing joy in the love of Christ, who rescues us from our sin, clothes us in his goodness, and is patient with us in our great weakness. Give us a vibrant and growing faith in you that quiets our minds and stills our greatest fears, so that we will be free to stop protecting ourselves. Give us a confidence in you that is so bold that we will move powerfully toward one another in honesty and love. In Christ's name, amen.

ASSURANCE OF PARDON: JOHN 14:6; 3:16–17

Jesus said to him, "I am the way, and the truth, and the life. No one comes to the Father except through me."

"For God so loved the world, that he gave his only Son, that whoever believes in him should not perish but have eternal life. For God did not send his Son into the world to condemn the world, but in order that the world might be saved through him."

HYMNS

"God, Be Merciful to Me"
"Wonderful, Merciful Savior"

SEXUAL IMPURITY

✥ CALL TO CONFESSION: EPHESIANS 5:5–10

For you may be sure of this, that everyone who is sexually immoral or impure, or who is covetous (that is, an idolater), has no inheritance in the kingdom of Christ and God. Let no one deceive you with empty words, for because of these things the wrath of God comes upon the sons of disobedience. Therefore do not become partners with them; for at one time you were darkness, but now you are light in the Lord. Walk as children of light (for the fruit of light is found in all that is good and right and true), and try to discern what is pleasing to the Lord.

✥ PRAYER OF CONFESSION

Loving heavenly Father,

We thank you for giving us faith to cry out to you for help. In our distress, you heard our cry and rescued us from ourselves and the punishment that we deserve. While we were still sinners, you brought us out of darkness into the light of your love and pleasure. We admit that our hearts should be overflowing with joy and gratitude to you all the time for this amazing privilege. Yet with our sinful natures, we still love darkness and choose to live in it. We regularly forget all that you have done for us and live lives driven by the many idolatries that grip our hearts and tempt our imaginations. Lord, forgive us for our great weakness and sin.

Father, we are full of sexual impurity. Our thoughts are given over to sexual fantasies and filling our minds and eyes with impure images, our hearts captured by romantic tales in which we control others and they worship us alone. Our hearts are devoted to using your gift of sexuality for our own pleasure and selfish benefit, instead of the holy purposes for which you designed it. We are unable to think sinlessly about sexuality, yet we deceive ourselves into thinking we are better than those who confess their sin openly. Father, forgive us for our sins, and for believing that they are too big to be forgiven by you. Forgive us for the pride and arrogance that magnifies sin and belittles your great work of salvation.

Lord, help us to walk as children of light. You have rescued us from darkness, and we thank you that we do not have to win your love through our obedience. Help us to become people who want to obey you because we are already loved by you in the fullest way. Draw us to meditate on the perfection of your Son, who never lifted his heart to an idol or gave himself over to sexual impurity in thought or action. Strengthen us to remember that his death and obedience have qualified us to share in his glorious inheritance, and may this truth dissolve our hard hearts with gratitude and melt our eyes to tears. Together, may we learn to walk in humble dependence on you day by day, trusting that your grace is sufficient for us to come boldly into your presence as cherished children. In Jesus' name, amen.

ASSURANCE OF PARDON: 1 CORINTHIANS 6:9–11

Do you not know that the unrighteous will not inherit the kingdom of God? Do not be deceived: neither the sexually immoral, nor idolaters, nor adulterers, nor men who practice homosexuality, nor thieves, nor the greedy, nor drunkards, nor revilers, nor swindlers will inherit the kingdom of God. And such were some of you. But you were washed, you were sanctified, you were justified in the name of the Lord Jesus Christ and by the Spirit of our God.

HYMNS

"Jesus, Thank You"
"Out of My Bondage, Sorrow and Night"

FOOLISHNESS

✣ CALL TO CONFESSION: EPHESIANS 5:15–17

Look carefully then how you walk, not as unwise but as wise, making the best use of the time, because the days are evil. Therefore do not be foolish, but understand what the will of the Lord is.

✣ PRAYER OF CONFESSION

Our wise and loving Father,

We come to you admitting our foolishness and habitual blindness to your will. We often believe that we are wiser and more loving than you are and seek to use prayer to manipulate you into doing what we want. We are full of turmoil and anxiety because we do not trust in your wisdom or believe that all your ways are best for us. Although we claim to believe in you and fear you, we spend most of our days living as though you do not exist. We rarely think of you or run to you with our cares and burdens, but instead frantically try to fix our problems according to our own foolish thinking. We forget to worship you throughout each day, because we cannot see your loving, sovereign kindness wrapped around us, even in our most painful moments. Father, forgive us.

Thank you for loving profoundly foolish and sinful rebels like us. You sent your cherished Son to live among blind and evil people, so that we could be rescued from our foolish depravity. He lived the perfect life of obedience and faith, demonstrating your wisdom for us in living proof with each word and action. On the cross he submitted to your gracious plan, choosing to pay for all our blind iniquity, sin upon sin. Now we stand before you as perfectly wise and righteous children, even though we will continue to struggle with blind foolishness until we see you face to face. For this we are eternally grateful.

Patient and persistent God, we thank you that we cannot change ourselves. If we could, we would take the credit for our discernment and despise brothers and sisters who were more foolish than us. Instead you have made us so completely dependent on you for every good thought and deed that we can only boast in you. Thank you for promising to complete the good work you have begun in us, even against our will. Please soften our hard hearts and open our blind eyes more each day. Help us to see you clearly, see our sin, and long to change. Keep us near the cross, always needy and looking to you for mercy and hope. Fill us with your wisdom and be our vision, our battle shield, our dignity and delight until we see you with new eyes. In Jesus' name, amen.

ASSURANCE OF PARDON: 1 CORINTHIANS 1:27–30

But God chose what is foolish in the world to shame the wise; God chose what is weak in the world to shame the strong; God chose what is low and despised in the world, even things that are not, to bring to nothing things that are, so that no human being might boast in the presence of God. And because of him you are in Christ Jesus, who became to us wisdom from God, righteousness and sanctification and redemption.

HYMNS

"Be Thou My Vision"
"It Is Well with My Soul"
"Jesus, Keep Me Near the Cross"
"No, Not Despairingly"

A NEW WILL

✥ CALL TO CONFESSION: PHILIPPIANS 2:12–13

Therefore, my beloved, as you have always obeyed, so now, not only as in my presence but much more in my absence, work out your own salvation with fear and trembling, for it is God who works in you, both to will and to work for his good pleasure.

✥ PRAYER OF CONFESSION

Great God of mercy and grace,

We confess how prone our hearts are to wander from you. Even though you interposed your precious blood to rescue us from the death our sins deserved, we still easily wander astray like lost sheep. Instead of reverently trembling in awe and wonder before you and pursuing holiness eagerly, we constantly turn aside after our idols, ignoring your life-giving statutes and the wise rules you have laid down for us in your Word. Our eyes covet the possessions you have given to our neighbors, as well as their bodies and their relationships. Our minds and our mouths are filled with unclean thoughts and words. Our hearts are set firmly on things that will rust, break, decay, and die, instead of being devoted to the one who loved us and gave himself for us.

Father, be at work in us more and more. Give us a new will that desires to obey you, then give us new strength to do the good things that you make us desire. When we do obey you, keep us from boasting, as if our new obedience were something we had accomplished by ourselves. When we fail, draw us into a deeper recognition of our utter dependence upon you and constant need of the gospel. Thank you for making us your people in Christ.

Jesus, thank you for perfectly working out your own salvation and ours. You revered your Father flawlessly while you lived here as a human being and delighted to obey all the statutes and rules in Scripture. Thank you for crediting that perfect obedience to us as if it were our own, and for preparing in advance good works for us to do as we imitate you.

Holy Spirit, transform our hearts by renewing our minds. Spread your holiness through every corner of our lives, so that we obey not out of slavish fear but out of joyful reverence for the God who has loved us so much. Teach us to see God's law as the perfect guide for our steps, and to revel in the freedom that is ours in Christ, who has taken away the law's threats by nailing them to the cross, making peace between us and God. Have your way within us according to your own good pleasure, as a potter shapes the clay for his own purposes. In Jesus' name, amen.

ASSURANCE OF PARDON: EZEKIEL 36:25–27

I will sprinkle clean water on you, and you shall be clean from all your uncleannesses, and from all your idols I will cleanse you. And I will give you a new heart, and a new spirit I will put within you. And I will remove the heart of stone from your flesh and give you a heart of flesh. And I will put my Spirit within you, and cause you to walk in my statutes and be careful to obey my rules.

HYMNS

"Come, Thou Fount of Every Blessing"
"Have Thine Own Way, Lord"
"How Deep the Father's Love"

PRESSING ON

✥ CALL TO CONFESSION: PHILIPPIANS 3:12–14

Not that I have already obtained this or am already perfect, but I press on to make it my own, because Christ Jesus has made me his own. Brothers, I do not consider that I have made it my own. But one thing I do: forgetting what lies behind and straining forward to what lies ahead, I press on toward the goal for the prize of the upward call of God in Christ Jesus.

✥ PRAYER OF CONFESSION

Heavenly Father,

How free and generous is your grace that reminds us of the spiritual dangers we face and urges us to press on to know and love you more. We thank you that though we often turn away from you in weakness and rebellion, you always draw us back to yourself. You welcome us even though we have nothing to commend us, and you forgive us for our many backslidings. Like the prodigal son, we are always wandering off into the far country, but you always welcome us back, dressing us in beautiful garments and rejoicing over us with great joy. We cannot comprehend such lavish love and forgiveness, but we thank you, for without it we would be utterly lost.

Jesus, though your robes of righteousness come freely to us by faith, they were purchased at unimaginable cost to you. You pressed on throughout your earthly life, steadfast in obedience and withstanding every attack from the evil one. You never wandered or faltered, even while suffering the deepest agony of rejection by your Father. Thank you for meriting our salvation, and for winning the greatest prize for us. You have paid the price for all our sin, past, present, and future, and you have wrapped us safely in the rich robes of your righteousness. We worship you, undone by your kindness and love.

Holy Spirit, hold fast to us. Melt our hearts with the powerful love shown to us at the cross. Fill our minds with its glory and attach our souls to the truths that we hear so often and yet so frequently forget. Hold us up, or we will fall time and time again. Show us truth, or we will follow after lies and worship false gods. Give us faith, or we will live in the barren wilderness of our own imaginations. Our every breath comes from you; give us abundant spiritual life and overflowing joy in the knowledge that you have made us your children and you will never let us go. In Christ's name, amen.

✥ ASSURANCE OF PARDON: ISAIAH 40:29–31

He gives power to the faint,
  and to him who has no might he increases strength.
Even youths shall faint and be weary,
  and young men shall fall exhausted;
but they who wait for the LORD shall renew their strength;
  they shall mount up with wings like eagles;
they shall run and not be weary;
  they shall walk and not faint.

✥ HYMNS

"Depth of Mercy"
"The Gospel Song"
"White as Snow"
"Who Is This?"

CONTENTMENT

✥ CALL TO CONFESSION: PHILIPPIANS 4:6

Do not be anxious about anything, but in everything by prayer and supplication with thanksgiving let your requests be made known to God.

✥ PRAYER OF CONFESSION

Redeeming heavenly Father,

You have surrounded us daily with your goodness and mercy. You have forgiven our sins, covered us in the shining robes of the perfect goodness of your Son, and protected our souls through every trial that you call us to endure. We should fill each day with praise, adoration, and thanksgiving to you, but we are weak, selfish, and full of sin. We love the gifts that you give us far more than we love you, and resent you when you call us to suffer. We get angry with you when you do not answer our prayers as we wish, and we wallow in anxiety and fear that you will take away the good things in our lives that we love too much. Forgive us, Lord, for doubting your love and goodness, and for finding joy and contentment in our own abilities, relationships, and possessions instead of in you alone.

Father, please rescue us from our discontented hearts. Thank you for Jesus, who endured deadly pain and suffering on our behalf, without ever giving in to anger, fear, or resentment toward you. He was truly content in every situation, finding joy and peace in you during each moment of his earthly life without grumbling or complaining. He had no earthly status or treasure, but valued your kingdom above all and never worshiped your creation instead of you. He trusted you completely, even when your plan took him to a brutal death, counting it joy to obey you. Thank you for the cross, for accepting his obedience in our place, and for giving us his record of perfect contentment and confidence in you.

Holy Lord, we desperately need your help to think pure and excellent thoughts about you and accurate thoughts about ourselves. Open our eyes to see your kindness in the midst of our suffering, and give us strong faith to believe that you love us when life is difficult. Remind us of the power of the cross, bathe us in the fountain of your forgiveness, and enrapture us with your beautiful Son. Steady our souls with pure, lovely, and noble truths about you, and grant us surprising peace as we cling to you, our Rock and our Redeemer. Make us patient and joyful though trials should come, utterly content in your love, and confident that your grace will bring us home. In Christ's name, amen.

✥ ASSURANCE OF PARDON: HOSEA 6:1–3

"Come, let us return to the LORD;
for he has torn us, that he may heal us;
he has struck us down, and he will bind us up.
After two days he will revive us;
on the third day he will raise us up,
that we may live before him.
Let us know; let us press on to know the LORD;
his going out is sure as the dawn;
he will come to us as the showers,
as the spring rains that water the earth."

✥ HYMNS

"Ah, Holy Jesus"
"Jesus, I Am Resting, Resting"
"The Power of the Cross"

KNOWING GOD'S WILL

✥ CALL TO CONFESSION: COLOSSIANS 1:9–10

And so, from the day we heard, we have not ceased to pray for you, asking that you may be filled with the knowledge of his will in all spiritual wisdom and understanding, so as to walk in a manner worthy of the Lord, fully pleasing to him, bearing fruit in every good work and increasing in the knowledge of God.

✥ PRAYER OF CONFESSION

Almighty, infinite Father,

As we come to you today to confess our weakness and rebellion against you, we thank you that you have chosen to love desperate sinners like ourselves. Your love and determination to rescue us from our sin give us the courage to admit the profound depravity of our desires, thoughts, and actions. We are people who want our kingdoms to come and our will to be done. Instead of pursuing spiritual wisdom with all our strength, we are delighted by our own wisdom and impressed with our own understanding. We despise your will, because it is so much stronger than ours and reminds us that we are not the gods we wish to be. We want to be worthy of your love instead of resting in the radiant worthiness of your Son. Father, forgive us.

Wonderful, merciful Savior, we thank you that you have disarmed the wrath of God. Though we are slow to bear fruit and prone to run far from you, you have paid for all our rebellion and weakness. By taking our sin upon yourself and giving us your perfect obedience, you have made us worthy to stand before God, confident that his justice is satisfied. Thank you for your nail-pierced hands, and for bearing all our sin and shame. In our weakness and sin we fall before your throne, praising and adoring you, for you alone are worthy.

Holy Spirit, our counselor, comforter, and keeper, remind us that while we live here on earth, we will continue to be weak sinners. In the midst of our many failures, give us joy in the cross and delight in our salvation. Humble us with our inability, and fill us daily with a fresh love for you that makes us long to delight you with our thoughts and actions. Please give us strong faith to believe that you are always for us and never against us, no matter how often we fall. When Satan tempts us to despair because of the profound sin that still entrances us, remind us that we have a Savior who stands before the throne of God interceding for us. Give us spiritual wisdom to behold our risen Lamb, perfect, spotless, and worthy to receive all our worship, adoration, and praise. In Christ's name we pray, amen.

✥ ASSURANCE OF PARDON: COLOSSIANS 1:11–14

May you be strengthened with all power, according to his glorious might, for all endurance and patience with joy, giving thanks to the Father, who has qualified you to share in the inheritance of the saints in light. He has delivered us from the domain of darkness and transferred us to the kingdom of his beloved Son, in whom we have redemption, the forgiveness of sins.

✥ HYMNS

"Depth of Mercy"
"I Will Glory in My Redeemer"
"Wonderful, Merciful Savior"
"Worthy Is the Lamb"

HEAVENLY MINDEDNESS

✣ CALL TO CONFESSION: COLOSSIANS 3:1–5

If then you have been raised with Christ, seek the things that are above, where Christ is, seated at the right hand of God. Set your minds on things that are above, not on things that are on earth. For you have died, and your life is hidden with Christ in God. When Christ who is your life appears, then you also will appear with him in glory.

Put to death therefore what is earthly in you: sexual immorality, impurity, passion, evil desire, and covetousness, which is idolatry.

✣ PRAYER OF CONFESSION

Almighty God,

We have come before you to worship you, but as we speak words of worship and sing songs of praise, we are reminded by your Word that we are to have no other gods before you. We have fallen woefully short of keeping this great command. Our worship of you is neither consistent nor wholehearted. You have called us to set our minds on things above, yet we habitually allow our minds to slip back toward things of earth: the fleeting pleasures that this world offers us in food, sexual immorality, and entertainment; the seeming glory it grants us in reputation, success, and money.

Lord Jesus Christ, we have often doubted that you could rescue our souls. We create elaborate systems of salvation to comfort ourselves in our desperate condition. Some of us have learned to live in blindness toward the sin that so easily ensnares us, assuming that we are better than we are and smugly satisfied that we are not like other sinners. Others of us have established rituals of self-hatred to cope with the sin that we find in our hearts, hoping that if we just work hard enough, you might find it possible to forgive our insidious and constant sins. One thing we have in common is that none of us sees our own sin clearly.

Instead we make too much or too little of it, and thereby obscure our view of your cross.

Holy Spirit, lead us back to the good news of the gospel: that all our sin has been put to death, fully and finally, by Christ on the cross. Help us to see the reality of our justification: we have been raised with Christ, and our relationship with God has been secured as beloved children. Help us to put to death the remaining sin in our hearts, but give us the confidence to admit that our struggle with sin is ongoing, and will be so until you glorify us. Give us bold faith that lingers at the cross longer than we linger over our sins. Entice us with the good news from above, so that our worship might flow from transformed hearts enraptured by a God who loved us first. Clear our spiritual vision, we pray, that we might see our souls as hidden with Christ on high, our Savior and our God. In his name we come, amen.

ASSURANCE OF PARDON: ISAIAH 12:1–3

You will say in that day:
"I will give thanks to you, O Lord,
  for though you were angry with me,
your anger turned away,
  that you might comfort me.

Behold, God is my salvation;
  I will trust, and will not be afraid;
for the Lord God is my strength and my song,
  and he has become my salvation."

With joy you will draw water from the wells of salvation.

HYMNS

"Before the Throne of God Above"
"Wonderful, Merciful Savior"

FORGIVENESS (3)

✥ CALL TO CONFESSION: COLOSSIANS 3:12–13

Put on then, as God's chosen ones, holy and beloved, compassionate hearts, kindness, humility, meekness, and patience, bearing with one another and, if one has a complaint against another, forgiving each other; as the Lord has forgiven you, so you also must forgive.

✥ PRAYER OF CONFESSION

Our God and our King,

We confess that we have a difficult time forgiving those who sin against us. Instead of putting on compassion and kindness, and forgiving as we have so richly been forgiven, we rehearse the sins of others and grow bitter and resentful toward them. We find it easy to judge people for their crimes against us, and hard to see that we sin in the same ways that they do, against you, against our friends, and against our families. We confess that we are easily confused about reconciliation. Sometimes in a rush to appear forgiving, we pursue people when our hearts are still full of anger, and we do damage with false claims of forgiveness and peace. At times we fail to trust people who deserve a second chance, while at other times we trust too quickly and give people further opportunities to sin against us. Lord, deliver us from our blindness and confusion, and help us to think clearly and lovingly.

Jesus, we thank you for entering our corrupt and sin-stained world so that we could be redeemed, forgiven, and reconciled to your Father. We did not value you or desire the inheritance you offered, but despised you, rebelled against you, and ran from you with all our strength. As nails were driven into your hands, you pled for the forgiveness of your tormenters. We too have crucified you. But you pursued us and rescued us, not only paying the great price of our forgiveness, but welcoming us into your family and seating us at your banqueting table. Thank you for your deep love for profound sinners like us.

Holy Spirit, we thank you that one day we will be completely reconciled and restored to all your people whom we have been unable to love and forgive in this world. Until then, give us wisdom to trust wisely, grace to forgive generously, and love to cover mountains of sin. We ask you to show us our sin, to comfort us with the gospel, and to give us grace to repent, forgive, and love people whom we cannot possibly love without your help. Oh God, as you have drawn us to yourself and not counted our sins against us, move us toward one another with joy and gratitude for how deeply we have been treasured in Christ. Amen.

ASSURANCE OF PARDON: LUKE 7:44–50; ROMANS 5:6, 9–10

Turning toward the woman [Jesus] said to Simon, "Do you see this woman? I entered your house; you gave me no water for my feet, but she has wet my feet with her tears and wiped them with her hair. You gave me no kiss, but from the time I came in she has not ceased to kiss my feet. You did not anoint my head with oil, but she has anointed my feet with ointment. Therefore I tell you, her sins, which are many, are forgiven—for she loved much. But he who is forgiven little, loves little." And he said to her, "Your sins are forgiven." Then those who were at table with him began to say among themselves, "Who is this, who even forgives sins?" And he said to the woman, "Your faith has saved you; go in peace."

For while we were still weak, at the right time Christ died for the ungodly. . . . Since, therefore, we have now been justified by his blood, much more shall we be saved by him from the wrath of God. For if while we were enemies we were reconciled to God by the death of his Son, much more, now that we are reconciled, shall we be saved by his life.

HYMNS

"All I Have Is Christ"
"Forgive Our Sins as We Forgive"
"Lord, at Your Table"

PEACE

✥ CALL TO CONFESSION: COLOSSIANS 3:15–17

Let the peace of Christ rule in your hearts, to which indeed you were called in one body. And be thankful. Let the word of Christ dwell in you richly, teaching and admonishing one another in all wisdom, singing psalms and hymns and spiritual songs, with thankfulness in your hearts to God. And whatever you do, in word or deed, do everything in the name of the Lord Jesus, giving thanks to God the Father through him.

✥ PRAYER OF CONFESSION

O God Most High,

Though we spend much time toiling, troubled, and distressed, you are forever at perfect peace. Your plans cause you no fear or anxiety; they stand as solid as the eternal hills. Your power knows no limits and your loving goodness no boundaries. You bring order out of our confusion, triumphing in our greatest defeats. As you rule over the intricacies of this universe, come and reign over the riot of our fearful hearts and minds. Though we should trust you, we are prone to walking through life with heavy hearts and chaotic minds. We worry about our health, finances, friendships, work, and families. We fret anxiously about losing all the good things you have given us, forgetting to thank you often. Father, forgive us.

Lord, we are fearful of our own sinful hearts. We make promises to you we can never keep, and fall into despair or bitterness when we cannot live up to our own expectations. When we try to obey you and fail, we fear your anger and disappointment, and are deeply embarrassed by our inability. When we are so weak that we don't even want to obey you, we wonder if we are Christians at all and run from you in shame. Father, give us peace with our weakness. Help us to accept the truth that as long as we live here on earth we will be depraved people wrestling with sin, yet bearing the glorious image of your Son, and safely sealed by his blood. Let us be unsurprised by our sin and depravity, but freshly astounded by your love for us in Christ.

Thank you for our precious Savior, who put off his glory and put on our sin so that we could put off our condemnation and put on his robes of joyful obedience. Show us Christ, walking through this chaotic and sinful world, bringing peace to creation, stilling waves, and quieting souls with equal ease. Show us Christ, receiving blows of shame in the greatest humiliation in all history, and enduring it with peace, confidence, and unswerving love for us. Show us Christ, forever standing before your throne, wearing our flesh and pleading for us, protecting and defending us. Oh God, melt our hearts with this truth until we delight to obey you, with hearts overflowing with thanksgiving and unshakable joy. In Jesus' name, amen.

✣ ASSURANCE OF PARDON: EPHESIANS 2:13–16

But now in Christ Jesus you who once were far off have been brought near by the blood of Christ. For he himself is our peace, who has made us both one and has broken down in his flesh the dividing wall of hostility by abolishing the law of commandments expressed in ordinances, that he might create in himself one new man in place of the two, so making peace, and might reconcile us both to God in one body through the cross, thereby killing the hostility.

✣ HYMNS

"Not What My Hands Have Done"
"Poor Sinner Dejected with Fear"

THE HEART

✤ CALL TO CONFESSION: HEBREWS 4:12–13

For the word of God is living and active, sharper than any two-edged sword, piercing to the division of soul and of spirit, of joints and of marrow, and discerning the thoughts and intentions of the heart. And no creature is hidden from his sight, but all are naked and exposed to the eyes of him to whom we must give account.

✤ PRAYER OF CONFESSION

Mighty God,

Your Word penetrates our hearts and exposes the truth about our thoughts and intentions. It uncovers our self-confidence and self-centeredness, as well as the secret sins that we hide so successfully from one another. The truth is that we cherish and love many evil thoughts in our hearts, even when outwardly we pretend to be full of spiritual desires. We harbor hatred and anger for those around us, along with jealousy and malice. We judge and condemn others in our hearts, or envy them and lust after them. Instead of loving our neighbor as we ought, we use our neighbors to feed our desires and passions. Even our good deeds are stained. We often wait to serve others around us until people are watching us, so that we may be admired and glorified. We speak your truth impatiently and without gentleness in order to prove ourselves. Father, forgive us not just for our sinful actions but for our corrupt and perverse hearts.

Jesus, thank you that you came to deliver us from our sinful self-centeredness. Your heart was always perfectly aligned with the Father's Word. Your thoughts as well as your actions were always pure and undefiled, filled with love for those around you and compassion for lost people. You worked hard in the Father's service, but you also rested confidently in the Father's power. Even though you are the Lord of Glory, eternally deserving of praise, you never glorified yourself. Instead you laid aside your glory and became a humble servant, defeating the forces of Satan through your own death, and winning victory in our place.

Holy Spirit, teach us not to trust in ourselves or in earthly sources of power and strength. Enable us to rest from all our attempts to win the Father's favor on our own, and to trust completely in Jesus, our great High Priest, who faithfully intercedes for us. Help us not to be unduly discouraged by the heavy load of guilt that so easily clings to our hearts. Instead, whenever we see clearly the sins of our hearts, enable us to fly to the truth of the Scriptures that in Christ the penalty of those sins has been paid for once for all. Remind us that we are now clothed in Christ's perfect righteousness, and that therefore there can be no condemnation left for us. In Christ's name, amen.

ASSURANCE OF PARDON: HEBREWS 4:14–16

Since then we have a great high priest who has passed through the heavens, Jesus, the Son of God, let us hold fast our confession. For we do not have a high priest who is unable to sympathize with our weaknesses, but one who in every respect has been tempted as we are, yet without sin. Let us then with confidence draw near to the throne of grace, that we may receive mercy and find grace to help in time of need.

HYMNS

"How Firm a Foundation"
"Laden with Guilt and Full of Fears"

HOLDING FAST TO OUR CONFESSION

✣ CALL TO CONFESSION: HEBREWS 4:14–16

Since we have a great high priest who has passed through the heavens, Jesus, the Son of God, let us hold fast our confession. For we do not have a high priest who is unable to sympathize with our weaknesses, but one who in every respect has been tempted as we are, yet without sin. Let us then with confidence draw near to the throne of grace, that we may receive mercy and find grace to help in time of need.

✣ PRAYER OF CONFESSION

Heavenly Father,

We confess before you today the weakness of our grip on our confession. In good times, we declare boldly that in Jesus we have a sympathetic High Priest, yet when trials and troubles come, we quickly feel abandoned and alone, convinced that you have forgotten us. Instead of drawing near to the throne of grace, full of confidence in your love for us, our hearts are consumed with frustration and fear. We lash out at those closest to us in anger, or withdraw within ourselves to sulk and hide. We run to the idols that promise us immediate escape or relief from our pain. We quickly forget that our merciful High Priest has ascended into heaven in triumph and intercedes for us there. As a result, we do not depend on you for the resources that we need in our weakness; we do not honor and revere you as the all-wise God who orders everything in the universe well, including our trials; and we do not obey you in our hearts or in our lives. Father, forgive us.

Jesus, thank you that you entered this world of suffering and temptation as our merciful and compassionate High Priest. You know what it is to be tired and overwhelmed; you know what it is to feel excruciating pain and weakness; you know what it is to be abandoned and betrayed. Thank you that you were faithful in all these things for us, holding fast to your confession, always trusting your Father, always revering him and obeying him from your heart. Thank you that you are completely without sin, and that you take away our filthy garments of distrust and disobedience and clothe us in your perfect and spotless holiness.

Holy Spirit, help us to cling on to our confession. Show us more clearly our eternal High Priest and Advocate above. Help us to ponder more deeply his love for us when we are tempted to doubt it. Intercede for us in our weakness, taking our incoherent prayers and presenting them perfectly before the Father. Strengthen us in growing holiness, as you continue in us the good work that you have already begun, so that on the last day we might be presented to Christ as part of his spotless bride, the church. In Jesus' name, amen.

✥ ASSURANCE OF PARDON: HEBREWS 7:23–28

The former priests were many in number, because they were prevented by death from continuing in office, but [Jesus] holds his priesthood permanently, because he continues forever. Consequently, he is able to save to the uttermost those who draw near to God through him, since he always lives to make intercession for them.

For it was indeed fitting that we should have such a high priest, holy, innocent, unstained, separated from sinners, and exalted above the heavens. He has no need, like those high priests, to offer sacrifices daily, first for his own sins and then for those of the people, since he did this once for all when he offered up himself. For the law appoints men in their weakness as high priests, but the word of the oath, which came later than the law, appoints a Son who has been made perfect forever.

✥ HYMNS

"How Sweet the Name of Jesus Sounds"
"Jesus, My Only Hope"

DEAD WORKS

✥ CALL TO CONFESSION: HEBREWS 9:13–14

For if the blood of goats and bulls, and the sprinkling of defiled persons with the ashes of a heifer, sanctify for the purification of the flesh, how much more will the blood of Christ, who through the eternal Spirit offered himself without blemish to God, purify our conscience from dead works to serve the living God.

✥ PRAYER OF CONFESSION

Living God,

We confess before you our deep attachment to dead works. We often seek to justify ourselves before you by our own obedience, even though the work of our defiled hands cannot be accepted into your holy presence. Sometimes we bind ourselves and others to do things in your name that you never commanded us to do. We think that by pursuing empty rituals or by denying ourselves things that you have declared good that you will somehow be pleased with us. At other times, we obey your Word out of a self-centered desire for our own glory and in order to declare our independence from you. We avoid small sins and pursue acts of righteousness that we find easy to perform, while blatantly ignoring far more important sins that have a strong grasp on our hearts. We denounce others for their inability to do these things, while ignoring the deep pride and lovelessness that pervade our lives. Father, forgive us.

Jesus, thank you for being our great High Priest. Thank you that as our representative you never offered your Father dead works. All your obedience came from a heart fixed on pleasing God. There was no pride or self-exaltation in your acts of service, nor were you selectively obedient in the commandments that you kept. Your hands and your heart were pure and clean as you offered a perfect and unblemished life of obedience in our place. You presented your own blood as the atoning offering that enables us to draw near to God with boldness.

Holy Spirit, give us confidence as we draw near to the throne of grace—not a confidence in ourselves and our own goodness, but a confidence founded upon Jesus Christ and his merits alone. Teach us to enthrone Christ in our hearts, and so be humbled; equip us to serve others out of the same mercy and grace that we ourselves have received. Give us the joy and gladness that comes from knowing that he has offered the once-and-for-all sacrifice in our place, and that he is returning again to be reunited with his people forever. In Jesus' name, amen.

✤ ASSURANCE OF PARDON: HEBREWS 9:24–28

For Christ has entered, not into holy places made with hands, which are copies of the true things, but into heaven itself, now to appear in the presence of God on our behalf. Nor was it to offer himself repeatedly, as the high priest enters the holy places every year with blood not his own, for then he would have had to suffer repeatedly since the foundation of the world. But as it is, he has appeared once for all at the end of the ages to put away sin by the sacrifice of himself. And just as it is appointed for man to die once, and after that comes judgment, so Christ, having been offered once to bear the sins of many, will appear a second time, not to deal with sin but to save those who are eagerly waiting for him.

✤ HYMNS

"Before the Throne of God Above"
"The Servant King"
"Sovereign Grace o'er Sin Abounding"

FAITHLESSNESS

✥ CALL TO CONFESSION: HEBREWS 11:1–3, 6; ROMANS 4:13

Now faith is the assurance of things hoped for, the conviction of things not seen. For by it the people of old received their commendation. By faith we understand that the universe was created by the word of God, so that what is seen was not made out of things that are visible.

. . . And without faith it is impossible to please him, for whoever would draw near to God must believe that he exists and that he rewards those who seek him.

✥✥✥

For the promise to Abraham and his offspring that he would be heir of the world did not come through the law but through the righteousness of faith.

✥ PRAYER OF CONFESSION

O Father of Jesus,

Help us to approach you with deep reverence and joyful faith, not with presumption or servile fear. Give us holy boldness and confidence that you are our faithful, covenant-keeping God, and that you cannot abandon or reject us. Forgive us, Lord, for we are not faithful followers of you. We confess that in religious duties, our lips and the feelings of our hearts have not always agreed. We have frequently taken your name carelessly on our tongues and trampled on your kindness with our many sins. We have desired and pursued things that would injure us, and have despised some of your chief mercies. We have harbored sinful hopes and fears, and we confess that we are unfit to choose for ourselves and direct our own steps. Like Esau, we are quick to exchange the glorious privileges of our birthright in Christ for the fleeting delights of sinful bodily pleasures. How can we ever thank you for your faithful patience with us, your very unfaithful children? Father, forgive us.

Lord Jesus, you have done all things well for us, your beloved brothers and sisters. In you there was no shadow of turning or faltering as you faithfully walked the path of obedience in our place. Though we are weak and inconsistent, you never change and you never will. You remain the same yesterday, today, and forever, and so our weak and faltering faith finds a strong and steady resting place in your perfect strength, goodness, and love. Jesus, thank you.

Holy Spirit, in unbelief we would stay far from you, hidden in fear and shame. Thank you for that faith, sometimes great and sometimes very small, which gives us entrance to your presence. Carry on your work, regardless of our stubbornness and apathy, and strengthen our weak faith until it strides forth in the great power of your name. Your Word is full of promises that are flowers of sweetest fragrance when gathered with discernment and faith. May we be made rich in faith, strong in its power, joyful in its sweetness, vigorous in its nourishment, steady in its source. Lord, increase our faith. In Christ's name, amen.

✤ ASSURANCE OF PARDON: ROMANS 4:2–3; 5:1–3

For if Abraham was justified by works, he has something to boast about, but not before God. For what does the Scripture say? "Abraham believed God, and it was counted to him as righteousness."

✤✤✤

Therefore, since we have been justified by faith, we have peace with God through our Lord Jesus Christ. Through him we have also obtained access by faith into this grace in which we stand, and we rejoice in hope of the glory of God.

✤ HYMNS

"Great Is Thy Faithfulness"
"I'll Rest in Christ"
"My Faith Looks Up to Thee"

RUNNING THE RACE

✣ CALL TO CONFESSION: HEBREWS 12:1–2

Therefore, since we are surrounded by so great a cloud of witnesses, let us also lay aside every weight, and sin which clings so closely, and let us run with endurance the race that is set before us, looking to Jesus, the founder and perfecter of our faith, who for the joy that was set before him endured the cross, despising the shame, and is seated at the right hand of the throne of God.

✣ PRAYER OF CONFESSION

Lord Jesus Christ,

Fill us with your Spirit today. We are running this race loaded down with sinful desires, idolatrous hearts, and mountains of guilt and shame that we pile on ourselves and each other. We confess to you that our frantic activity springs more from strategies of self-salvation than from real sorrow over sin and love for you. Our running takes us far away from the forgiveness, peace, and rest you freely give us. Train our hearts to run to you instead of away from you. Forgive us for all our desperate attempts to save ourselves.

Fill us with your Spirit so that we become preoccupied with his work and presence. We are fascinated with our small lives and blind to your larger purposes; send him to open our blind eyes and make us see your will, your heart, your beauty, and your glory. May he give us faith to see our names engraved on your hands, our souls redeemed by your blood, and our mountains of sin leveled by your life of pure obedience. Send your Spirit as our comforter to cheer us in our sorrow and failure. Send him as the searcher of our hearts to show us our own deceitfulness and helplessness so that we will hate our sin, run to you, cling to you, and rest on you as the beginning and end of our salvation.

Wonderful Savior, we long to worship you with pure hearts and lives, yet we cannot live without sinning. In this life we will never escape our deep need for your mercy; help us to cherish it richly and transform us by it. May your love and kindness captivate our minds and imaginations, strengthen our weak faith, and motivate us to leave behind the sins that so easily entangle us. You have won the race for us; now run it with us day by day, moment by moment, and fix our eyes on you instead of on ourselves. For yours is the majesty, the glory, and the kingdom forever and ever, amen.

ASSURANCE OF PARDON: HEBREWS 10:19–22

Therefore, brothers, since we have confidence to enter the holy places by the blood of Jesus, by the new and living way that he opened for us through the curtain, that is, through his flesh, and since we have a great priest over the house of God, let us draw near with a true heart in full assurance of faith, with our hearts sprinkled clean from an evil conscience and our bodies washed with pure water.

HYMN

"Depth of Mercy"

TRIALS

✥ CALL TO CONFESSION: JAMES 1:2–6

Count it all joy, my brothers, when you meet trials of various kinds, for you know that the testing of your faith produces steadfastness. And let steadfastness have its full effect, that you may be perfect and complete, lacking in nothing.

If any of you lacks wisdom, let him ask God, who gives generously to all without reproach, and it will be given him. But let him ask in faith, with no doubting, for the one who doubts is like a wave of the sea that is driven and tossed by the wind.

✥ PRAYER OF CONFESSION

Guiding Father,

Forgive us for our lack of faith. As you called Abraham out of his country into unknown circumstances, so you often call us to walk through frightening, lonely, or unstable times. In response to trials of various kinds, we have certainly not counted them as joy. Like sheep, we are prone to wander at these times; we have turned—every one of us—to our own way. In moments of suffering, we have looked for wisdom from this world, comforting ourselves with man-made schemes to deal with our suffering or escaping into addictive patterns of numbing behavior. Our vision for what you are doing in our lives in the midst of suffering is blindingly clouded by fear and anger, and we have consistently settled for our own limited, self-centered vision as the final word of truth.

Yet in your immeasurable grace, the Good Shepherd has laid down his life for his selfish, wandering sheep. Holy Jesus, thank you for the life of doubtless faith that you lived on our behalf. You came from heaven to take on human flesh and live perfectly in the place of your children. In the midst of every kind of trial and temptation, you responded with utmost trust and faith in your Father's will. Even as your Father turned his face away as you were crucified for our sin of unbelief, you remained faithful, to your final breath, declaring your atoning work as finished. What vast, free, abounding grace!

Spirit of God, bind our wandering hearts to you as we walk through the paths that you have ordained for us. When we suffer, be our vision by teaching us to count this cost as joy and strengthening our belief that you always have redemptive purposes in the suffering of your children, as we see so clearly in the cross of Christ. Enable us to cry out for wisdom when we lack it, and humble us to see that we lack wisdom often. Grow our faith in the promise that you will not leave us as we pass through troubled waters, that we will not be burned when we are called to walk through fire, and that we do not need to fear, for you have called us by name; we are yours. In Jesus' name, amen.

ASSURANCE OF PARDON: JOHN 10:7–11; 16:33

So Jesus again said to them, "Truly, truly, I say to you, I am the door of the sheep. All who came before me are thieves and robbers, but the sheep did not listen to them. I am the door. If anyone enters by me, he will be saved and will go in and out and find pasture. The thief comes only to steal and kill and destroy. I came that they may have life and have it abundantly. I am the good shepherd. The good shepherd lays down his life for the sheep."

"I have said these things to you, that in me you may have peace. In the world you will have tribulation. But take heart; I have overcome the world."

HYMNS

"Ah, Holy Jesus"
"Be Thou My Vision"
"Come, Thou Fount of Every Blessing"
"Grace Unmeasured"
"I Am the Lord Your God"

REPAYING EVIL FOR EVIL

❖ CALL TO CONFESSION: 1 PETER 3:9

Do not repay evil for evil or reviling for reviling, but on the contrary, bless, for to this you were called, that you may obtain a blessing.

❖ PRAYER OF CONFESSION

O God,

We come before you as people who desperately need to see you with clear vision. We need to behold your majestic glory and feel our smallness; we need to gaze upon your awesome holiness and feel our sinfulness; we need to see Jesus' humble self-offering at the cross and feel how truly loved we are. Father, as we gaze upon your beauty, help us to see how unlike you we really are. We eagerly repay evil to those who have done evil to us and revile and mock others who revile or mock us; when we are unable to lash back effectively at those who have caused us pain, we feel frustrated and angry. You, however, have loved us while we still hated you; you spoke words of peace to us while we used your name as a curse; you have richly blessed us, even as we continue to look anywhere and everywhere else for our blessings.

Lord Jesus, you know exactly how it feels to receive undeserved evil. You were mocked and beaten for us: when sinful men reviled you, you were silent like a sheep before its slaughterer; when people cursed you, you spoke words of forgiveness and blessing in return. Thank you for living the life of unmatched goodness that we should have lived, and for taking our place under the curse that our sin merits.

Holy Spirit, help us to live lives that are truly a blessing to those around us. Help us to love those who are unkind and unfair to us, to speak kind words to those who mock us, and to be gentle with those who are harsh. Thank you that your declaration of blessing upon us is sure and unmovable, rooted and grounded in your unchanging and eternal character. In Christ's name, we pray, amen.

✣ ASSURANCE OF PARDON: EPHESIANS 1:3–6

Blessed be the God and Father of our Lord Jesus Christ, who has blessed us in Christ with every spiritual blessing in the heavenly places, even as he chose us in him before the foundation of the world, that we should be holy and blameless before him. In love he predestined us for adoption as sons through Jesus Christ, according to the purpose of his will, to the praise of his glorious grace, with which he has blessed us in the Beloved.

✣ HYMNS

"Behold Our God"
"Come Ye Sinners"
"Hail to the Lord's Anointed"

HUMILITY

✥ CALL TO CONFESSION: 1 PETER 5:6–7

Humble yourselves, therefore, under the mighty hand of God so that at the proper time he may exalt you, casting all your anxieties on him, because he cares for you.

✥ PRAYER OF CONFESSION

Loving Father,

We come to be humbled by your mighty truth, and pray that you will grant us a deeper understanding of ourselves, our sin, and our Savior. We confess now that we have often failed to wait for you to exalt us, but have instead felt sure that we must do this for ourselves. We have stewed in anxiety, quietly and secretly doubting that you care for us. When friends fail us, or we are misunderstood or purposely attacked by others, we have been left feeling empty and worthless, not made whole by your love for us. When we are tempted and tried, we often fail. When we fail, we do not look to the good news that Jesus has already won our victory over sin and death and is our present strength in weakness. When our hearts are breaking, we quickly escape to what most pleases our flesh, rather than turning to the comfort of our souls.

The depth of your mercy is truly astounding. Thank you for sending Jesus to live perfectly on the behalf of his chosen ones, including broken, proud, and anxious people like us. That he would choose to humble himself to take on flesh is difficult for us to understand. That he would willingly, for the joy set before him, endure the agony of crucifixion and separation from you, is beyond our comprehension. Lord, help us to see the joy with which he pleads for us before your throne. Help us to remember that his unending, saving, wondrous love will not let us go.

Our Refuge, please cause us to run to the cross as we continue to struggle with our remaining sin. Make us aware of our own patterns of pride and anxiety. Help us to ask for help. Grant us the humility of approachability, and the courage to speak words of loving confrontation to our comrades around the cross. In all things, lift our eyes to the saving, helping, keeping love of our wonderful Savior, in whose name we boldly come, amen.

ASSURANCE OF PARDON: 1 PETER 5:10–11

After you have suffered a little while, the God of all grace, who has called you to his eternal glory in Christ, will himself restore, confirm, strengthen, and establish you. To him be the dominion forever and ever. Amen.

HYMNS

"Depth of Mercy"
"Jesus, What a Friend for Sinners"
"O Love That Will Not Let Me Go"
"Thy Mercy, My God"

SACRIFICIAL LOVE

✥ CALL TO CONFESSION: 1 JOHN 4:7–11

Beloved, let us love one another, for love is from God, and whoever loves has been born of God and knows God. Anyone who does not love does not know God, because God is love. In this the love of God was made manifest among us, that God sent his only Son into the world, so that we might live through him. In this is love, not that we have loved God but that he loved us and sent his Son to be the propitiation for our sins. Beloved, if God so loved us, we also ought to love one another.

✥ PRAYER OF CONFESSION

Glorious God,

We praise you for the privilege of knowing you. We have lived in this world, yet often have been ignorant of its Creator; we have enjoyed your tender care without knowing you as the provider. In blindness we have enjoyed sunlight, and we have listened to voices all around us while profoundly deaf to spiritual truth. We have understood many things without knowledge of your ways, and have seen the world yet failed to see Jesus. We live each day as sovereigns of our own kingdoms, carrying out our desires and bending others to our wills. Instead of submitting humbly to those you have called us to obey, our souls rise up with prideful indignation, inflamed with desires for self-determination. We fear that if we love others sacrificially, we will lose the world, and so we fight for our kingdom to come and our will be done. Father, forgive us for our sin, and for the great damage we do to others as we sin.

Lord Jesus, you have entered into the darkness of our world in order to possess us and save us. You submitted to the will of your Father, loving us sacrificially as you carried our cross up the hill of execution and died in our place. With your perfect obedience and death, you have crushed the head of the serpent forever and wrapped us in the silken robes of your righteous submission and sacrificial love. In losing yourself, you gained the treasure for which you longed: our salvation. Jesus, thank you.

Holy Spirit, grant that we may weep in praise of the mercy that we have found. May we tell others as long as we live that you are a pardoning God who pursues proud and selfish sinners and transforms them into grateful, humble, loving, and sacrificial saints. Though we are weak in this life and only make small beginnings in obedience, may our hearts expand with joy to think of the great treasure that is ours in Christ. His perfect love casts out our fear, for though we continue to sin, there is no condemnation left for us, and an eternity of joy has been purchased by his blood. Give us boundless gratitude and increasing grace to live in submission to your perfect and loving will, and to sacrifice ourselves as he laid down his precious life for us. In Christ's name, amen.

✥ ASSURANCE OF PARDON: ROMANS 5:17, 2, 1

If, because of one man's trespass, death reigned through that one man, much more will those who receive the abundance of grace and the free gift of righteousness reign in life through the one man Jesus Christ.

✥✥✥

Through him we have also obtained access by faith into this grace in which we stand, and we rejoice in hope of the glory of God.

✥✥✥

Therefore, since we have been justified by faith, we have peace with God through our Lord Jesus Christ.

✥ HYMNS

"All I Have Is Christ"
"Jesus, Priceless Treasure"

INDEX OF THEMES

INDEX OF CALLS TO CONFESSION

INDEX OF ASSURANCES OF PARDON

INDEX OF SERMON TEXTS FOR WHICH THE PRAYERS WERE WRITTEN

INDEX OF MUSICAL RESOURCES

In our worship service, the prayer of confession and assurance of pardon are followed by hymns and songs related to their themes. Often the prayers of confession themselves allude to these songs, or to others used elsewhere in the service. The following is a list of the hymns and songs that we sing, keyed to particular prayers. Hymns are identified where possible with reference to *The Trinity Hymnbook*, revised ed. (Suwanee, GA: Great Commission, 1990).

"Abide with Me" (*TH* 402). Henry Lyte, 1847. 148–49

"Ah, Holy Jesus" (*TH* 248). Johann Heermann, 1630. 76–77, 142–43, 192–93, 212–13

"Alas, and Did My Savior Bleed." Words: Isaac Watts, 1707; additional words and music: Bob Kauflin © 1997 Sovereign Grace Praise (BMI). 24–25, 88–90

"All I Have Is Christ." Jordan Kauflin © 2008 Sovereign Grace Praise (BMI). 40–41, 62–63, 80–82, 98–99, 114–15, 150–51, 152–53, 178–79, 180–81, 198–99, 218–19

"All My Heart This Night Rejoices" (*TH* 217). Paul Gerhard, 1653. 18–19, 100–101

"Always Forgiven." Jonathan Baird and Ryan Baird © 2003 Sovereign Grace Worship (ASCAP). 32–33

"Amazing Grace (My Chains Are Gone)." John Newton, Chris Tomlin, and Louie Giglio © 2006 Sixsteps Music (EMI Christian Music Publishing). 30–31, 102–3, 156–57

"And Can It Be" (*TH* 455). Charles Wesley, 1738. 118–19, 156–57

"Arise My Soul Arise." Words: Charles Wesley, 1742; music: Kevin Twit © 1996 Kevin Twit Music (ASCAP). 20–22, 44–46

"Depth of Mercy." Words: Charles Wesley, 1740; additional words and music: Bob Kauflin © 1998 Sovereign Grace Praise (BMI). 26–27, 124–25, 128–29, 160–61, 190–91, 194–95, 210–11, 216–17

"Forgive Our Sins as We Forgive" (*TH* 494). Rosamond Herklots, 1969. 178–79, 198–99

"From the Depths of Woe" (Psalm 130). Christopher Miner © 1997 Christopher Miner Music. 36–37, 60–61, 62–63, 96–97, 108–9

"God, Be Merciful to Me." Words: *The Psalter*, 1912; music: Christopher Miner © 1998 Christopher Miner Music. 110–11, 122–23, 168–69, 182–83

"Gospel Song, The." Words: Drew Jones; music: Bob Kauflin © 2002 Sovereign Grace Praise (BMI)/Sovereign Grace Worship (ASCAP). 190–91

"Grace Unmeasured." Bob Kauflin © 2005 Sovereign Grace Praise (BMI). 24–25, 66–67, 106–7, 212–13

"Great Is Thy Faithfulness" (*TH* 32). T. O. Chisholm, 1923. 208–9

"Guide Me, O Thou Great Jehovah" (*TH* 598). William Williams, 1745. 68–70, 160–61

"Hail to the Lord's Anointed" (*TH* 311). James Montgomery, 1821. 214–15

"Hark! the Herald Angels Sing" (*TH* 203). Charles Wesley, 1739. 114–15

"Have Thine Own Way, Lord" (*TH* 688). Adelaide Pollard, 1907. 188–89

"He Was Wounded for Our Transgressions" (*TH* 244). Thomas Chisholm, 1941. 92–93

"Hide Away in the Love of Jesus." Steve Cook and Vikki Cook © 2008 Integrity's Hosanna! Music (ASCAP)/Sovereign Grace Worship (ASCAP). 110–11, 136–37, 140–41

"His Forever." Words: J. G. Small, 1863; additional words: Pat Sczebel © 2003 Sovereign Grace Worship (ASCAP). 92–93